Street Smart Trivia

日英対訳

日本のギモン

日刊ゲンダイ＝編
ジョンソン　スティーヴンリン＝訳

装　　幀＝岩目地 英樹（コムデザイン）
カバーイラスト＝テッド・高橋
編集協力＝Michael Brase

※ 本書は、弊社刊『対訳ニッポン双書　街中のギモン』を改訂・再構成したものです。

Copyright© 2015 Nikkan Gendai
All rights reserved.
Originally published in Japan by KODANSHA, Tokyo.
English translation rights arranged with KODANSHA, Japan.

Street Smart Trivia

日英対訳

日本のギモン

日刊ゲンダイ＝編
ジョンソン スティーヴンリン＝訳

IBCパブリッシング

Part 1 社会システムのギモン
Problems with the Social System

婚姻届はなぜ24時間受け付けているのか?　　12
Why does city hall accept marriage applications 24 hours a day?

渋滞の長さはどうやって測るのか? 　　16
How do they measure the distance of traffic jams?

高速道路の料金係はどうやって交代しているのか? 　　20
How do people working in expressway toll booths change shifts?

指名手配犯にかけられた懸賞金ってホントにもらえるの? 　　24
Can you really get the reward money shown on wanted posters for turning in a criminal?

道路の案内標識に書かれている距離はどこを基点に測っている? 　　28
What point do they use to measure the distances displayed on highway direction signs?

偽札を警察に届け出るとどうなる? 　　32
What happens if you turn in counterfeit money to the police?

「宮内庁御用達」はどのように決められる? 　　36
Who decides what's "By appointment to His Majesty the Emperor"?

信号待ちの時間が場所によって違うのはなぜ? 　　40
Why does the time it takes for the traffic signal to change vary by location?

なぜ青信号なのに緑色? 　　44
Stop on red; go on . . . blue?

● CONTENTS

なぜ男子の大会に女子選手が出場できるのか？   48
Why can women athletes compete in men's competitions?

「不快指数」はどうやって決めているのか？   52
How do they calculate the "discomfort index"?

紙にはなぜAとBの2サイズがあるのか？   56
Why does paper come in A sizes and B sizes?

歩道をふさいで商品の搬入。警察は許可してるのか？   60
Is it legal for delivery trucks to park on the side walk while making their deliveries?

通話料無料の110番。誰が料金負担してるのか？   64
It's free to call the police on 1-1-0; but who actually foots the bill?

持ち主が現れない忘れ物のカサはどうなるのか？   68
What happens to all those forgotten umbrellas?

ゴミの分別方法はなぜ地域によって違う？   72
Why do the garbage separation rules vary from area to area?

国会図書館にエロ本はあるのか？   76
Do they keep any dirty books at the National Diet Library?

同じ番地なのに電柱の住所表示の色が違う？   80
Why are the addresses on telephone poles displayed in different colors, even at the same address?

降水確率はどうやって決めている？   84
How is the "chance of precipitation" calculated?

紙幣の視覚障害者用「点字マーク」が消えた!?   88
What? No more denomination indicators for the blind on the new yen bills!?

なぜ水道料金だけ2ヵ月ごとの請求なのか？　　　　　　　**92**
Why does the water bill only come once every two months?

再生紙は何回くらい"再生"されるのか？　　　　　　　　　**96**
How many times is recycled paper actually "recycled"?

Part 2　街中のギモン
Problems in the Town

「皇居の周りを走るジョギングはなぜ左回り？　　　　　　**100**
Why does everyone jog around the Imperial Palace counterclockwise?

神社にはなぜ玉砂利が敷かれているの？　　　　　　　　**104**
Why do so many Shinto shrines use pea gravel to pave their grounds?

お札の肖像画は誰が描いている？　　　　　　　　　　　　**108**
Who draws the portraits printed on our money?

露出過剰はどこまで見せたら罪になる？　　　　　　　　**112**
How much exposure is indecent?

「猛犬注意」の札の効果は!?　　　　　　　　　　　　　**116**
Do "Beware of Dog" signs really do any good?

街頭の占い師。資格はいるのか？　収入は？　　　　　**120**
Do sidewalk palm-readers have some kind of qualification? How much do they make?

おみくじはなぜどこの神社でも同じなのか？　　　　　　**124**
Why are *omikuji* fortunes the same at all the Shinto shrines?

道路のトンネル照明にオレンジと白があるのはなぜ？　　128
Why do highway tunnels have both orange and white lighting?

セーラー服が減っている理由は？　　132
Why are sailor suit uniforms on the decline?

郊外の駅前のたこ焼き屋はだれでもできるのか？　　136
Can anyone set up a *takoyaki* stand out in front of a train station?

水族館の海水はどこから運んでいる？　　140
Where does aquarium water come from?

エスカレーターで右側を空けて乗るのはなぜ？　　144
Why do people keep the right side of the escalator open?

Part 3 鉄ちゃんのギモン
Problems with Trains

電車のシート、1人当たりの幅の基準は？　　150
What's the standard for deciding how many people should fit into that train seat?

駅構内のチャイム音は何を知らせているのか？　　154
What are those chime sounds for that you hear in train stations?

東京駅に向かうのが「上り」列車とは限らない!?　　158
Not all trains heading for Tokyo are "inbound"?

電車に書かれた記号の意味は？　　162
What do the serial numbers on train cars represent?

終電後の駅員はどうやって帰るのか？ **166**
How do train station employees get home after the last train has left?

新幹線の乗車率はどうやって調べているのか？ **170**
How do they calculate passenger boarding rates on the shinkansen?

Part 4　生活のギモン
Problems with Daily Life

氷屋の氷と家庭の氷はどこが違うのか？ **176**
Is there any difference between ice you get at an ice shop and ice you make at home?

なぜコーヒーはスチール缶でビールはアルミ缶なのか？ **180**
Why does coffee come in steel cans and beer in aluminum?

代々木の「々」は何と読む？ **184**
What's that "character" you use to repeat kanji called?

なぜ男物と女物のシャツは打ち合わせが逆？ **188**
Why do men's and women's shirts button up on different sides?

「なるべくお早めにお召し上がりください」とは何日？ **192**
"Consume quickly." Could you be more specific?

洋服の「フリーサイズ」とは、どういう基準？ **196**
Exactly what size is "one-size-fits-all?"

「1万円入りま〜す」の意味は？ **200**
"¥10,000 going in!" Do you have to tell the world?

● CONTENTS

コンドーム自動販売機が銭湯の隣にあるのはなぜ？　204
Why are there condom vending machines next to public bathhouses?

理美容院で切り落とした髪の毛はその後どうなるのか？　208
What happens to all the hair that gets cut at the hairdresser's?

銀行や役所でなぜ「シヤチハタ」はダメ!?　212
Why can't "Shachihata" stamps be used at banks and public offices?

なぜ暮れに"第九"が演奏されるのか？　216
Why does it all end with Beethoven's Ninth?

ペットは何を飼ってもいいのか？　220
Are you allowed to keep anything as a pet?

ちぎれた1万円札、銀行で交換してくれるのか？　224
Can you really exchange a torn ¥10,000 bill at the bank?

なぜペットボトル入りの牛乳はないのか？　228
Why don't they sell milk in plastic bottles?

緊急車両は任意保険に入っているの？　232
What kind of insurance do emergency vehicles have?

ざるそばはノリをのせただけでなぜあんなに高いのか？　236
Why is *zaru soba* so expensive when it's only garnished *nori*?

Part 1

社会システムのギモン

Problems with
the Social System

婚姻届は なぜ24時間受け付けているのか?

　婚姻届は早朝でも夜中でも役所の夜間窓口で受け付けてくれる。お役所の24時間サービスというのも珍しいが、そもそもどうして婚姻届は24時間受け付けなのだろうか。

　「婚姻届は、24時間受け付けが行われています」と言うのは法務省。死亡者の**配偶者**は**遺産**の少なくとも半分を相続できるが、生前に婚姻届を出していなければ配偶者になれない。24時間受け付けになっているので、いつでも相続の権利が得られるようになっている。

　「**相続**に関しては、死亡が先か婚姻届が先かで事情が全く違います。婚姻は届け出があって初めて成立するので、24時間受け付けにしないと、死亡と婚姻届の前後関係が相続争いの原因になりかねないんですよ」(法務省)

　婚姻届を提出すると、役所は受付年月日を記録する。後に審査されて初めて正式受理となるが、正式

社会システムのギモン ● Problems with the Social System

Why does city hall accept marriage applications 24 hours a day?

City offices in Japan will accept **marriage applications** at the "night window" in the wee hours of the morning and at the latest hours of the night. Twenty- four-hour-a-day service is a rare thing from the government, so what's the deal with marriage applications?

"Yes, we accept marriage applications 24 hours a day," says the Ministry of Justice. When a person dies, the **spouse** is entitled to at least half of that person's **estate**, but if no marriage application is ever filed while that person is still alive, there is no way they could ever have had a spouse. So that's why marriage applications are accepted 24 hours a day: so you can always be sure to inherit what you're entitled to.

"When it comes to **inheritance**, the question of which came first, the death or the marriage application, can change everything. Marriage is only officially recognized once a marriage application is filed, so accepting the applications 24 hours a day helps to ensure that there's no fighting when it comes time to divide a person's estate, by making it clear whether the marriage was official while the deceased was still alive." (Answer by the Ministry of Justice)

When a marriage application is submitted, the city office records the date it was brought in. The marriage isn't actually

受理されれば、婚姻届の受付日が婚姻の「成立日」になる。死にかけの資産家を前にした**内縁の妻**が遺産をほしいと思ったら、夜中でも早朝でも、とにかく死ぬ前に婚姻届を出せば遺産獲得というわけだ。

離婚問題などに詳しい山口宏弁護士が言う。「遺産がらみでなくても、男が夜中に酔った勢いで"おまえと結婚してやる！"なんて調子よくハンコを押して、考え直す間もなく婚姻届を出してしまう、なんてことも24時間受け付けでは起こります。もちろん、それでも婚姻は成立です」

実は、**戸籍法上の届け出**はすべて24時間受け付け。離婚届でも同じことが起こり得る。酒気帯び状態で夜中に夫婦げんかなんかした日には、何が起こるかわからない!?

お役所の「24時間サービス」は遺産相続のからみからだった！

"Night window" entrance sign at the Shinjuku Ward Office in Tokyo.

recognized until an investigation can be completed, but afterward, the official "date of marriage" becomes the date the application was filed. So if you find your **common-law spouse** on their deathbed, whether it's the wee hours of the morning or the middle of the night, you'd better get your marriage application filed as soon as possible—before the person dies, in any case—if you want your cut of the estate.

According to Hiroshi Yamaguchi a lawyer specializing in divorce cases, "It isn't just all about inheritance issues. Suppose two lovers are drinking and in the heat of passion and/or drunkenness decide, "Let's get married!" and they fill out the application and put their seals* to it, and one of them takes it to the "night window" while the other is passed out, they'll have big news waiting when they wake up in the morning... "Sorry, but you're married now."

In fact, 24-hour-a-day service is available for all matters relating to **family registries**, so the same thing could happen when it comes to divorce. So be careful if you've been out drinking and gotten into an argument with the unhappy spouse who was waiting for you at home. You never know what might happen!

Translator's Note: *In Japan, a "seal," is a kind of personal stamp, used to make documents official; similar to how a signature is used to make a document official in the West.

渋滞の長さは
どうやって測るのか？

　帰省シーズンには、「**渋滞40キロ**」「次のICまで3時間」などという渋滞情報をよく目にする。この渋滞の長さはどうやって測っているの？　もしかして長～いメジャーで測るとか？

　「高速道路の下に埋め込んである"トラフィックカウンター"という機械を使って距離を**測定**しているんです」と言うのは、東名、名神、中央道などの高速道路を管轄する中日本高速道路㈱の広報担当者。日本道路公団は2005年10月に東日本、中日本、西日本の3社に分割されたが、高速道路の渋滞測定システムは各社基本的に共通だという。では、そのトラフィックカウンターとはなんぞや？

　「道路の地下5メートルから10メートルの深さに埋められた**電磁線**の呼び名です。この上を車が通ると、車両の数はもちろん、大きさ、速度まで計測できるんですよ」（中日本高速道路広報室）
　トラフィックカウンターは道路の縦方向に5.5メートルの間隔をあけて2つ埋められている。そこで生まれる時間差から、車両の速度や、それが普通車なのか

社会システムのギモン ● Problems with the Social System

How do they measure the distance of traffic jams?

During the summer holidays, you often see displays reading "**TRAFFIC JAM** 40 KM" or "3 HRS TO NEXT INTERCHANGE" on the highway. How do they measure the length of congested traffic? Don't tell us there's someone out there with a really long tape measure...

"We use devices called 'traffic counters' which are buried beneath the expressways to **measure** the distance," is the answer we got from the press office of Central Nippon Expressway Company Limited, which manages the Tomei, Meishin, and Chuo Expressways. In October 2005, the Japan Highway Public Corporation was privatized and divided up into the East Nippon, Central Nippon, and West Nippon Expressway Companies, but the system they use to measure traffic congestion is the same for each company. So then, what's the deal with these "traffic counters"?

"That's the name for the **electromagnetic lines** buried between five to ten meters beneath the expressway. When vehicles pass over, we can measure not only the number of cars, but also their size and how fast they're traveling."

Traffic counters are planted in pairs with a vertical distance of 5.5 meters between them. Based on the differences in the readings generated by each member of the pair, the speed

17

大型トラックなのかが分かるのだそうな。なかなかの優れモノらしいが、これでどうやって渋滞の距離が分かるのだろう。

「このトラフィックカウンターは、例えば東名高速道路なら2キロごとに設置してあります。私どもでは、車の速度が40キロ以下の状態を渋滞とみなしているのですが、それが連続して2カ所で検知されれば4キロ、3カ所で検知されれば6キロの渋滞、となるわけです」（中日本高速道路広報室）

連続20カ所なら渋滞40キロというわけ。このデータをもとに**目的地**までの所要時間なども計算される。こうした情報は交通管制センターに集められ、そこから道路上の交通情報板やVICSセンターに送られ、FM電波などを介して各ドライバーに伝えられる。

では、夏休みや年末に帰省する時の「高速道路」利用のアドバイスを。

「当たり前ですが、やはり混む時間を避けることが一番ですね。"ドライブカレンダー"や"ハイウェイナビゲーター"をぜひ活用してください」（中日本高速道路広報室）

これらはいずれも東日本、中日本、西日本各社のホームページから閲覧できる。渋滞をうまく**避けて**、楽しいドライブを！

as well as weight of vehicles passing by can be measured. That's rather impressive technology, but how does this information get converted into traffic jam lengths?

"For example, in the case of the Tomei Expressway, there is a pair of traffic counters planted every 2 km. So if we detect any speed less than 40 km/h (our official definition of 'traffic jam,') for two consecutive pairs of counters, then we know we have 4 km of congestion; less than 40 km/h for three consecutive pairs, then 6 km of congestion, etc."

So if "traffic jam" speeds are detected at 20 consecutive pairs of counters, then—you guessed it—you've got a traffic jam 40 km long. Based on this data, the time it will take to reach various **destinations** it calculated and the information sent out to electronic displays along the expressways and at rest areas, and also to radio stations.

But don't you have any advice for how to avoid traffic jams in the first place?

"Unfortunately, the best advice we can give is just to try to avoid the times when the roads are most crowded. But taking advantage of our 'Drive Calendar' and 'Highway Navigator' services can also be helpful." (Answers by the press office of Central Nippon Expressway)

These services can be accessed on each of the East, Central, and West Nippon Expressway homepages. **Stay away from** traffic jams, and enjoy your drive!

高速道路の料金係は
どうやって交代しているのか？

　車が高速で行きかう道路を渡るのは危険きわまりない。そのうえ高速道路は車両以外進入禁止だから**歩道**もない。もちろん、人が歩くことはできないはず。では、料金所の係員はどうやって交代しているのだろうか？

　東日本高速道路㈱に聞いてみたところ、関越自動車道で一番交通量の多い新座料金所（埼玉県）を見学させてくれた。ここには入り口、出口あわせて16の料金所ブースがある。

　それぞれのブースの近くに出入り口があり、階段を下りると地下通路につながっている。通路は高さ3メートル、全長90メートル。高速道路の下を横断しており、係員は詰め所からこの通路を通って交代している。

　料金所の係員は2時間交代で勤務。苦労が多い仕事だ。

　窓を開け放しているため**排ガス**をモロに受けることはご存じのとおり。中から外に向かって空気を吐き出すエアカーテンは設置されているが、かつては2時間も勤務すると、服やイスが真っ黒になったとか。

社会システムのギモン ● Problems with the Social System

How do people working in expressway toll booths change shifts?

What could be more dangerous than trying to cross an expressway? Cars speed by, and since they're only made for cars, of course there are no sidewalks... So how are the poor folks who work in the toll booths supposed to get in and out of there?

We decided to inquire with East Nippon Expressway Company Limited, and they let us have a tour of the Niiza Toll Station, in Saitama Prefecture, the busiest **toll station** on the Kan-Etsu Expressway. Here, there are a total of 16 toll booths serving drivers getting on and off the expressway.

Each booth has its own staircase leading to an underground passageway. The passageway is 3 meters high and 90 meters long, spanning the entire width of the highway, and this is how workers make their way to and from the break room when it's time to change shifts.

Toll booth employees work on shifts only two hours long. It's a tougher job than you might imagine.

They have to leave the windows of the booth open the whole time they work, so you can imagine how much **exhaust fumes** they are exposed to. There are now air curtains in place to prevent too much of these gases from getting inside the booth, but in the past, after only two hours on the job, their

「ETCや東京都の**ディーゼル規制**でだいぶましになりました」(同料金所係員)

とはいえ、ETC搭載車が専用レーンと一般レーンを間違った際に、車を誘導するため道路に下りた係員が車にひかれる不幸な事故も起きている。

また、カードの入れ間違いなどETCのエラーでバーが閉まり、急ブレーキをかけた車に後続車が追突する事故も急増しているそうだ。

「ETCを使う際はカードがちゃんと入っているか確認して、料金所には時速20キロ以下で入ってください」(東日本高速道路広報)

便利なETCが事故頻発の原因にもなっているとは皮肉な話だ。

uniforms as well as the stools they sat on would become black with the soot of the exhaust.

"Things have gotten a lot better with the introduction of ETC (Electronic Toll Collection) and the Tokyo Metropolitan government's **restrictions on diesel vehicles**," one employee told us.

But ETC hasn't been all good news. If an ETC-equipped car makes a mistake between the ETC lane and a regular lane, booth attendants have to get out of the booth to guide them around to the ETC lane, putting them in great risk of getting hit by other cars on the highway.

Also, if drivers don't have their ETC cards set in place properly, the gate arms won't open as they pass through the lane, causing them to slam on the brakes and increasing the risk of getting hit from behind.

"When you use ETC, always make sure you have your card properly set in place and slow down to at least 20 km/h as you pass through the toll gate," says East Nippon Expressway's press office. ETC may make driving the expressways more convenient, but what good is it if it's just going to cause more accidents!

指名手配犯にかけられた懸賞金ってホントにもらえるの?

交番や駅に**指名手配**のポスターが張ってある。中には懸賞金がかけられているものも。本当に懸賞金をもらえるのだろうか?

たまたま見かけた指名手配には200万円の懸賞金がかけられていた。まずは近所の交番のおまわりさんに聞いた。

「だれが懸賞金を出しているのですか?」と質問すると、「ええ、被害者の会だと聞いています」との返事。

「本当に200万円もらえるのですか?」

「もちろん。ちゃんとお金はしかるべきところで保管しているはずです」

念のため指名手配のポスターに記された**フリーダイヤル**に電話してみた。

おまわりさんにしたのと同じ質問をした。すると担当者は、「だれがお金を出しているのかは言えません。情報提供以外の電話は一切受け付けていません」とケンもホロロの対応であった。

これでは情報提供しても懸賞金がもらえるのかどうかはわからない。そこで、旧知の弁護士に聞いた。

社会システムのギモン ● Problems with the Social System

Can you really get the reward money shown on wanted posters for turning in a criminal?

We often see posters showing **wanted criminals** in the train station or in front of police boxes, often boasting hefty reward money for assistance with the criminal's capture. But after the police get their criminal, are they really going to give you all that money?

We happened upon a wanted poster offering a reward of ¥2 million. So we headed for the nearest police box and decided to ask:

"Who is offering all that reward money?"

"Uhh, I heard it's some kind of victims' association," we were told.

"Are they really going to shell out ¥2 million?"

"Of course, I'm sure they've got the money properly set aside."

Not satisfied, we decided to try calling the **toll-free number** listed on the wanted poster, and asked the same question we asked the police officer.

"We can't say who is providing the reward money. This number is only to provide information about the whereabouts of the criminal," the operator scolded us coldly.

Well, with that kind of attitude, how could we ever be sure we'd get our reward money if we decided to help them in the

彼は笑いながら「だれが懸賞金をかけているかはコメントしにくいだろうね。狙われる恐れがあるから」と言ったあと、次のように付け加えた。
「懸賞金が本当にもらえるかどうかも難しいよ」

　つまり、情報を提供したとしても本当にその情報が犯人の検挙に結びついたかどうかの判断はきわめて難しく、支払いをめぐってトラブルになる可能性も十分だという。

　とはいえ、現実は2001年に大阪の会社員の**ひき逃げ事故**で犯人が逮捕された際、**情報提供者**に200万円の懸賞金の一部が支払われている。懸賞金がもらえるかどうかはケース・バイ・ケースといえそうだ。

いったい、だれがお金を出しているのか？
Who on earth is picking up the tab for this?

first place! Next, we tried inquiring with an old lawyer friend of ours.

"Of course, they're not just going to tell you where the money's coming from," he chuckled. "If their identity were public, they'd be easy targets for anyone who doesn't want to see the criminal caught. In any case, there's really no way you could be sure of how much reward money you'd be able to get, if any."

Basically, even if you do provide information, there's a very good chance you would have a hard time getting a piece of the reward money, because it can be very difficult to decide how much the specific information you provided contributed to the criminal's arrest.

Be that as it may, when the criminal in the 2001 **hit-and-run** death of an Osaka company worker was recently arrested, the **informant** actually did receive a portion of the offered ¥2 million reward. So it seems that whether you will be actually rewarded for crime-fighting, civic-mindedness can only be decided on a case-by-case basis.

道路の案内標識に書かれている距離はどこを基点に測っている？

道路の案内標識には「東京 23 km」などと書かれているが、この場合、東京都のどこまでの距離を表示しているのか？

車を運転している時には便利な案内標識。「11 km」「26 km」など、やけに半端な数字が記されているから、おおよその目安というよりは具体的な地点までの距離なのだろう。例えば「厚木 26 km」とあった場合、厚木市に足を踏み入れる地点、つまり市境まで26キロという意味なのだろうか。案内標識を管轄している国土交通省に聞いてみた。

「市町村名と距離が表示されている場合、記されている数字は、通常、各市町村の役所の正面地点までの距離です」（国土交通省道路局企画課）

高速道路上で「大阪 57 km」と記されていたら、高速道路を降りて大阪市役所前まで主要道路を通っていった場合の距離が57キロという意味だ。ただし、「東京 ○ km」に限っては、道路原点である日本橋までの距離を表示しているのだという。

社会システムのギモン ● Problems with the Social System

What point do they use to measure the distances displayed on highway direction signs?

We always see direction signs on the highways reading, for example, "TOKYO 23 KM," but where exactly in the metropolis is it that they're measuring these 23 km from?

These convenient direction signs give us fairly accurate-seeming figures, like "11 KM" or "26 KM," not exactly round numbers, so there must be some specific point from which they're measuring these distances. For example, if we see "ATSUGI 26 KM," does that mean that it's 26 km until we'll first set foot in Atsugi—the distance from the sign to Atsugi city limits? We decided to ask the Ministry of Land, Infrastructure and Transport, which **has jurisdiction over** highway signage.

"In cases where the distance is displayed next to the name of a city or town, the distance is measured from that location to the main entrance of the city hall of the destination in question." (Answer by the Ministry of Land, Infrastructure and Transport's planning department)

So if you see "OSAKA 57 KM" on the expressway, that means that if you get off the expressway and take the most standard route up to the front door of Osaka City Hall, the distance will be 57 km. The only exception is Tokyo, for which distances are measured not from city hall, but from

また、街中では「日比谷 10 km」「巣鴨 13 km」など、市町村以外の地名が案内されている標識も見かけるが、これはどこを基点にしているのか？
「駅などのランドマークや、その地名を冠した主要**交差点**を基準にしています」（同企画課）

　ところで、**一般道路**の案内標識は「青地に白文字」、高速道路の案内標識は「緑地に白文字」だが、表示方法も異なることをご存じだろうか。同方向の複数地名が案内されている場合の並び順が逆なのだ。

　一般道路では、上を向いた矢印で現地点からの遠近感を表しているため、遠い地名ほど上（矢印の先側）になっているが、高速道路の案内標識は近い順に上から書かれている。**降りるインター**を見逃すことがないように、近い地名を最上段にしているそうだ。

Nihonbashi, which is the point of origin for all roads leading to the capital.

But we also see signs in the city reading, for example, "HIBIYA 10 KM" or "SUGAMO 13 KM," indicating location-names other than cities. What about these? "These signs measure the distance from the main train station, major **intersection**, or other landmark," the planning department tells us.

As a side note, you might be aware that direction signs on **surface roads** are written in white on a blue field, while direction signs on the expressways are written in white on green; but did you know that the place names on the signs are listed in different orders as well?

On surface roads, an upward arrow is used to indicate distance from that location, so the farther the destination, the further up (direction of the arrow) it's name appears on the sign. But on the expressways, destinations are listed with the nearer distances appearing first. This is thought to help people from missing their **off-ramp** by listing the nearest place names at the top.

偽札を警察に
届け出るとどうなる？

1万円札を**自販機**で使おうと思ったら使えない。よく見たら偽札だった！ なんて場合、銀行や警察に届けるとどうなるか。交換してもらえるのだろうか?

警察庁のまとめによると、2004年の1月から5月までに発見された**偽札**は、1万2578枚と過去最悪のペース。精巧な偽札も出回っていて、知らないうちに偽札を手にする可能性は十分にある。自分で偽造したものでなくても、偽札と知って使用すれば刑法(148条)違反の重罪だ。どうすればいいのか。日本銀行に尋ねてみた。

「疑わしい銀行券をお持ちいただければ鑑定をいたしますが、偽造券とわかった場合、お返しして警察に持っていってもらいます。私どもでは交換・返金はいたしておりません。あとは警察の**管轄**ですので……」(日本銀行政策広報)

ならば最初から警察に持っていったほうが話が早い。届け出ると、どうなるか。警察庁広報室に聞いた。

社会システムのギモン ● Problems with the Social System

What happens if you turn in counterfeit money to the police?

"Why won't this **vending machine** take this ¥10,000 bill? Let's have a look... Oh, my God! It's counterfeit!" If such a thing were to happen to you, what do you think would happen if you took it to the bank or to the police? Would they exchange it with a new bill for you?

According to the **National Police Agency's** figures, 12,578 **counterfeit bills** were discovered in circulation between January and May 2004. That's the highest figure from any five-month period in the agency's history. With so many hard-to-detect counterfeit bills floating around, you can never be sure that one of them won't make its way into your hands. Even if you didn't make it yourself, knowing use of counterfeit money is a serious crime (Article 148 of the Criminal Code). So what should you do?

According to the Bank of Japan's press office: "We'll perform an appraisal to confirm the authenticity of any suspect bill brought to us, but if it turns out to be counterfeit, we have to return it to you and ask that you take it to the police. We cannot perform any kind of exchange or refund. The matter is entirely under the **jurisdiction** of the police..."

In that case we might have saved ourselves the hassle by taking it to the police directly! But what will happen after the

「偽札は届け出人の了承を得て、任意提出を求めています。同額紙幣との交換は行っておりません」

押収されてしまうとは**踏んだり蹴ったり**。
「謝礼金を支払う制度はあります。昭和52（1977）年に『偽造通貨発見届け出者に対する協力謝金制度』が設けられ、捜査協力の内容、その程度に応じて謝礼金を支払うことになっています」（同広報室）

謝礼金の具体的な額はケース・バイ・ケースで一概には言えないが、「届けた紙幣の額に見合った相応の金額」とのこと。ただし、すでに解決済み案件にかかわる偽札だった場合、「捜査に役立たない」ため、謝礼金は一切出ない。

知らずに手にした偽札なのに没収されて終わりじゃ、まるっきり届け損だ。届け出ずに、素知らぬ顔で使ってしまいたくなるが……。なんとも理不尽な話だ。

police get their hands on it?

"We ask for people who discover counterfeit money to turn it in voluntarily. There's no exchange for new bills," says the National Police Agency's press office.

Talk about adding insult to injury!

"There is however the possibility or receiving a 'reward,'" they continue. "The 'Counterfeit Discovery Cooperation Reward System' was established in 1977 to reward people for cooperation with counterfeiting investigations as well as resulting arrests."

But the "results" of a person's cooperation with an investigation are weighed differently case by case, so it's hard to put even a rough figure on how much of a reward you can expect. The best answer we were able to get was: "a comparable sum to the face value of the counterfeit money turned in." However, if the counterfeit bills you turn in happen to be connected to a case that's already been solved, then there's no "cooperation with the investigation," and you're out of luck.

"So if it isn't my fault I got this counterfeit money, what good is it going to do me to turn it in and possibly be out of the cash all together?" Our poor victim at the beginning of this story might think. "Might as well just pretend I never noticed anything and try to use it!" Hmmm, it does make you think . . .

「宮内庁御用達」はどのように決められる？

　名店・老舗と呼ばれる店の中には「**宮内庁御用達**」という看板を掲げ、宣伝文句にしているところが少なくない。「宮内庁御用達」のお墨付きは、どのようにすればもらえるのだろうか？

　宮内庁報道室によれば、「『御用達制度』は現在は存在しません」とのこと。すでに廃止されているのだ。

　明治24（1891）年に生まれた「御用達制度」は、もともとは商工業を奨励するために生まれたもので、5年間にかぎり有効だったそうだ。

　主にお菓子、しょうゆ、砂糖などの「宮内庁に出入りする業者」で、「社会上の相当の信用を有するもの」が選ばれた。衛生管理などのチェックはもちろん、一説には家庭環境や、病歴、思想歴などを2親等にまでさかのぼって調査する厳しい審査が行われたという。

　昭和24（1949）年の契約を最後に事実上廃止され、それ以降、宮内庁は「御用達制度」を公式には認めていない。

　「戦後諸制度が変わる中で、**自然消滅的**になくなっ

社会システムのギモン ● Problems with the Social System

Who decides what's "By appointment to His Majesty the Emperor"?

Several of the long-established Japanese houses of business display signs reading "**By Appointment to His Majesty the Emperor**" and use the slogan as a kind of advertisement for their businesses. But who controls the use of this title?

According to the press office of the **Imperial Household Agency**: "Currently, there is no appointment to His Majesty." The system was done away with long ago.

The "Appointment System" was established in 1891, with an initial validity of only five years, with the intention of promoting commerce and industry.

At that time, companies which could boast to have earned "a high degree of trust from society" were chosen mainly from makers of candies, soy sauce, sugar, and other "goods consumed by the royal family." Of course, their quality controls were subject to scrutiny, but some sources even report the domestic situations, histories of illness, and even political beliefs of these companies' owners having been subject to check—as far as two generations back.

The last contract bearing this "appointment" officially ceased to be valid in 1949, and the Imperial Household Agency hasn't officially recognized the system since. "After WWII, many of the ways we operate changed, and the system

ていきました。はっきりした事情はわかりません」(宮内庁報道室)

しかし、今でも「宮内庁御用達」の看板を掲げている店はある。中には言ったもの勝ちとばかりに、皇室関係者が一度だけ訪れたような店が勝手に名乗っているケースもあるようだ。

「『御用達制度』があった時期に許可された業者が、今日なお看板などに表示していることがあるのは承知していますが、社会通念に照らして**不当な**理由でなければ、かつて許可されたものという経緯もあるので、宮内庁としては黙認しています」(同報道室)

形骸化しているとはいえ、「宮内庁御用達」という言葉には威厳とありがたみを感じてしまうもの。「不当な使い方をしている場合には注意を与えている」(同報道室)そうで、勝手に名乗っちゃいけないのだ。

なんと、昭和24年で廃止されている!
Defunct since 1949.

just seemed to **die out naturally**. No one, however, can say for certain why," says the Agency's press office.

Nonetheless, a good number of businesses continue to insist upon their "appointments." There are even a few who have no connection at all with the original system at all. The best justification they can give for their advertising practice is that some member of the imperial family visited their shop once.

"For businesses which were approved while the system was still in place, the Agency doesn't particularly mind their continuing to use the slogan, as long as it's not being used in a way which would be **detrimental** to the welfare of society," the press office tells us.

So even though the system of "appointment to his Majesty" has become a **dead letter**, no one can deny that the slogan still carries a good deal of weight and is respected by the Japanese public. But what's to be done about businesses who use the slogan unfairly? The best answer the Imperial Household Agency could give us is: "We give them a warning."

信号待ちの時間が場所によって違うのはなぜ？

街を歩いたり車で走るとき、必ずお世話になるのが**信号**である。

赤になったり青になったり規則的に変わるが、場所によってインターバル時間は異なる。いったいだれがどうやって決めているのか？

記者が疑問に思ったのは、次のようなことからだ。駅から自宅までの間に**押しボタン式の信号**が2つある。そのうち交通量の多い道路にある信号はボタンを押してから変わるまでに1分ほどかかる。もう1つの交通量の少ないほうはボタンを押すとすぐに信号が変わり、渡れるのだ。

近所の警察に聞いたところ、「システムはいろいろありますが、基本的には2通りです」という返答。

1つは近くの**時差式の信号機**と連動させるため、ボタンを押しても近くの信号が変わるまで待たせる方法。言うまでもなく渋滞を起こさせないための配慮だ。

もう1つは近くに時差式の信号がない場合で「30

社会システムのギモン ● Problems with the Social System

Why does the time it takes for the traffic signal to change vary by location?

You can't get away from **traffic signals**, whether you make your way through town on foot or by car. Of course, they all change regularly from red to green and back, but the time it takes for the light to change can vary depending on the location. Who decided this, and how do they decide the interval of time? Here's what particularly caught one of our writers' attention about this question: From his home to the station, he has to cross two **push-button crosswalks**. One is on a busy thoroughfare, and it takes about one minute from the time you push the button for the signal to change. The other is on a less busy street, and the signal changes soon after you push the button.

We decided to ask at the local police station.

"There are various systems in place to control traffic signals, but basically they fall into one of two groups," we learned.

The first type works in coordination with the nearest major traffic signal running on a timer. With this type of signal, even if you push the button, the signal won't change until the main **timed signal** changes. This is, of course, necessary to keep traffic running smoothly.

In the other type, if there is no timed signal nearby, the

分〜1時間の間に押した人がいないとすぐに変わります。少し前に押した人がいると30秒くらいは待つことになりますが」という。なるほど。では、赤や青の継続時間はだれがどうやって決めるのか?

「地元の警察署の交通課で決めます。交差点だったら、四方の交通量をはかり、どちらの方向は"青を何秒にする"といった具合に」

信号機には「制御機」が付いていて、それに時間をセットすることによって交通課の計画したとおりに信号の色は変わっていくという。「渋滞が多いので信号のシステムを変えてほしいなんていう苦情があったら?」と聞いた。
「調べて、必要があると判断すれば変更します」

ただし、制御機の中をいじって設定を変えるのは素人にはムリ。業者を呼んでシステムを修正してもらわねばならないのだという。記者は勝手に「大掛かりにコンピューター制御しているのだろう」と思っていたが、現実は信号機ごとに時間を設定していることがわかった。
「制御機だけで250万円くらいするのですよ」と言っていたが、けっこう高いものなんだナ。

signal changes right away unless "someone else has already pushed the button in the last 30 to 60 seconds. If the signal had already just changed for someone else, then you'll probably have to wait about 30 seconds for it to change for you."

That makes sense. But what about the time intervals for the main timers? Who decided these, and how?

"They're set by the traffic division of the local police. They measure the amount of traffic in each direction at the intersection, and then decide how much time to allow for each green signal."

The signals are equipped with control boxes which are set with the appropriate intervals to keep the signals changing **in accordance with** the police's findings.

"What do you do if people **complain about** traffic jams and ask you to change the signal timing?" we asked.

"We do an investigation, and if we find there's a better way to set the intervals, then we change the settings in the control box."

However, not just any police officer can go in and change the control box settings. A special engineer has to be called in to **adjust** the system. Our writer had assumed that there was some computer system controlling a whole network of signals, but **it turns out that** each major intersection runs on its own control box, which has to be set independently.

We also learned that one control box costs ¥2,500,000. So we hope the police do call the engineer before they mess with things themselves!"

なぜ青信号なのに緑色？

信号機の青信号の色、文字通り青色のものと、青というより緑色に近いものが混在しているのに気づく。青信号なのになぜ緑色？

「青信号で使える**色の範囲**に幅を設けているからです。色を数値化してグラフ表示した"色度図"をもとに、使用可能範囲を警察庁で定めています」（警察庁交通規制課）

たしかに色度図で青信号の使用可能範囲を見ると、水色に近い青からホウレンソウのような緑までかなり幅が広い。色がほぼ決まっている赤信号や黄信号に比べ、かなりあいまいだ。

「実はもともと"進め"を表す信号は"緑信号"でした。昭和5（1930）年に日本で初めて東京・日比谷に信号が設置されましたが、そのとき定められた法令でも"緑色信号"と明記されています」（同交通規制課）

英語で「グリーンシグナル」というように、国際的にも"ゴー"は緑色。CIE（国際照明委員会）でも、交通信号の色は「赤・黄・緑」としている。

「ところが、いつの間にか人々は緑信号を"青信号"

Stop on red; go on . . . blue?

At some point, every student of Japanese has to accept that green no longer means "go." A green traffic light is called an *ao shingo* (lit. "blue signal"). And if you've lived in Japan for a while, you may notice that the color of a "green" light can vary from actual green to dark bluish-green. So what's the story?

According to the traffic regulation division of the National Police Agency, "You see a **range of hues** in the traffic lights because there is a 'range' of color which we define as acceptable, based on arithmetic color representations."

And when they showed us some samples of what's acceptable, the "range" was wide indeed, with some hues bluish green and others as dark green as a leaf of spinach—a much wider range than what is specified for yellow or red.

"Originally, the color for 'go' in Japan was 'green' as well," we learned. "When Japan got its first traffic signal in 1930, in Hibiya, Tokyo, the law of the day literally referred to a 'green signal.'"

So is this a peculiarity of Japan alone? What about other countries? The CIE (International Commission on Illumination) also defines the colors for traffic signals as "red," "yellow" and "green"—not blue.

According to traffic signal manufacturer Kyosan Electric

と呼ぶようになりました。日本では昔から緑色を"青"と呼ぶ習慣がある。青菜や青葉、青リンゴがいい例です。語呂のよさも手伝って、青信号の呼び名が定着していったようです」(信号機メーカー大手の京三製作所)

　昭和22 (1947) 年に施行された道路交通取締令でも、実態に合わせて「青信号」という名称に変えられた。そのため、緑っぽい色をしていても「青信号」と呼ばれ続けてきたのだ。昭和47 (1972) 年には、地方ごとにバラバラだった信号の色に統一基準をつくり、青っぽい色も使えるようになった。以降、信号機は緑と青が混在するようになったのだという。

　また、**色弱者**は赤と緑が判別しにくいので、青寄りの色も使えるようにした、という背景もあるようだ。

白黒写真だと「青」が右か左か一瞬戸惑う（答えは左）

Seen in black and white, can you tell which is green (or blue)? Answer: Left.

Mfg. Co. Ltd., "Somewhere along the way, people just started calling the green light 'blue.' But in Japanese, we often use the word 'blue' (*ao*) for things that when you stop to think about it are actually green, like green vegetables (*aona*), green leaves (*aoba*), and green apples (*ao ringo*). It also probably helped that *ao shingo* is less of a mouthful than *midori shingo*. Eventually, it just became part of the language."

In the Traffic Enforcement Act of 1947, the law was made to reflect actual speech, and the wording was changed to *ao shingo*, and that has been the official name ever since, no matter how *midori* it may actually look. And when standards were drawn up in 1972 to regulate traffic signals, which at that time varied greatly from region to region, bluish hues were also included in the specifications, giving the range of colors we see today.

The fact that **color-blind people** have trouble distinguishing between green and red is also said to be one of the factors considered.

なぜ男子の大会に女子選手が出場できるのか？

　このところ男子のプロゴルフ大会に女子選手が出場しているのを**見かける**。ほかのスポーツでも男子の大会に女子が出ることは可能なのか？

　ゴルフの場合は団体によって規定が違う。日本ゴルフ協会では男子の大会は男子のみ、女子の大会は女子のみが原則だという。

　日本ゴルフツアー機構と日本プロゴルフ協会では特に「女子が出てはいけない」という規定がなく、**原則的には**予選を通るなどの実力があれば男子の大会に出場できる。しかし大会によっても細かい出場規定があって一概には言えないとのことだ。

　その他のスポーツではどうか。例えばプロ野球には選手を男子に限る規定はなく、実際に**入団テスト**を受けた女子選手もいる。社会人野球も大学野球も男女の区別はない。唯一、高校野球だけが出場選手資格を「男子のみ」と定めている。

Why can women athletes compete in men's competitions?

Recently, we **witness** women trying their hand in men's pro golf tournaments. Are women atheletes allowed to compete in men's tournaments in other sports as well?

In the case of golf itself, the rules depend on the group holding the tournament. The Japan Golf Association clearly specifies men's tournaments as being only for men, and women's tournaments only for women.

But for the Japan Golf Tour and the Japan Professional Golfers' Association, there's no rule excluding the participation of women; so **in principle**, if a player is able to make his or her way through the preliminaries, they are welcome to participate in the final "men's tournament," regardless of sex. However, this isn't a general rule since there are further regulations, depending on the tournament in question.

How about with other sports? For example, in the case of professional baseball, there is actually no rule at all dictating it should be a "man's sport," and it isn't unheard of for women ballplayers to show up for a team's **try-outs**. For semi-pro baseball and college baseball as well, there is no regulation to prevent women's participation. High school baseball is the exception, with regulations clearly stating that sanctioned games are for "boys only."

日本サッカー協会のチーム登録資格は、年齢による第1種から第4種、シニア、女子と分かれているが、Jリーグや大学リーグなどが含まれる第1種には、女子が参加してはいけないという規定はない。チームごとの事情にもよるが、**理論上**は女性Jリーガーが誕生する可能性もあるのだ。

　出場資格のうえでは、意外と男女の壁は低い。しかし、スコアで競うゴルフは別にして、体力差がモノをいう競技で男女が真剣勝負をするのはやはり非現実的か。スポーツ評論家の谷口源太郎氏も「そもそも近代スポーツにおいて男女が競い合うという概念はないし、今後もないだろう。ただし男子のシンクロ、女子の硬式野球など、互いの領域に進出し合うことは今後もあると思う」と言う。

　ちなみに男女の区別がまったくないのは**馬術**。馬を操る技術や感性に負う割合が高いからで、競技によっては女子のほうが**有利**というものもあるそう。

社会システムのギモン ● Problems with the Social System

The Japan Football Association divides its organization of teams as Class 1 through Class 4, depending on age, plus separate groups for seniors and women. But for Class 1, which includes the Japan Professional Football League (J. League) and college leagues, there is no rule barring women from playing. So circumstances may vary depending on the team, but **in theory** the day may come when we'll see women J. Leaguers on the pitch.

So as far as regulations go, the barriers against women in sport are fewer than you might have imagined. But unlike golf, in most sports the requirements of physical strength make the differences between men and women somewhat more difficult to overcome. In the words of sports critic Gentaro Taniguchi, "The entire idea of men and women competing together is foreign to the concept of modern sports to begin with, and it's probably not a trend that we'll see develop much further. I do believe, however, that we can expect to see both men and women creating their own competitions in sports that have traditionally been dominated by the other sex, for example, a pro women's baseball league, or men's synchronized swimming."

An interesting case of a sport which makes no distinction between men and women whatsoever is **equestrianism**. In fact, many argue that women are **at an advantage** in the sport because of the delicacy and sensitivity required to control the horse.

「不快指数」はどうやって決めているのか？

夏になると天気予報などでよく聞かれるのが「**不快指数**」だ。

不快指数90％なんて聞くとそれだけで暑苦しくなるというものだが、いったい、だれがどうやって決めているのか。かつては地震の震度も人間の**体感**で決めていたというから、もしかして「あ～今日は一段と暑いから90％ね」なんてふうに、気象予報士の「不快感」で決められてたりして？

気象庁に聞いてみた。

「そんなことはありませんよ。不快指数にはちゃんと決まった計算式があるんです。ただし不快指数を発表しているのはうちではありません」（**気象庁**広報室）

実は気象庁では、不快指数をはじめ、洗濯指数やゴルフ指数などの生活気象情報は、「情報の有効性が低い」という理由で一切発表していないのだ。それらはすべて気象庁のデータをもとにした民間気象予報会社の手によるもの。

How do they calculate the "discomfort index"?

You know it's summer in Japan when the weather forecaster wraps things up with an announcement of the day's "**discomfot index**" (also known as the "temperature-humidity index"). When we hear "Today's discomfort index, 90%," we know we're in for a hot and humid one, but how exactly do they arrive at these figures. Just as the seismic intensity scale used to be actually based on people's **perceptions** of an earthquake, does the weather forecaster just "feel" like, "Oh, today's a lot hotter than yesterday so we'd better move it up to 90," and make an announcement?

"No, no, not at all," the press office of the Japan **Meteorological Agency** informs us. "There is a proper formula for calculating the discomfort index, but we're not the ones who calculate it."

In fact the Agency doesn't calculate any of the various "indices" you hear from time to time on the weather report, such as the "laundry index" (to let you know whether your clothes are going to dry during the rainy season) or the "golf index" (to let you know how suitable tomorrow is going to be for a day around the links,) as it deems such information to be "of little validity." These are all calculated by private weather forecasters, based on the Meteorological Agency's data.

ただし不快指数の求め方はあらかじめ決まっている。その計算式は〈0.81×気温＋0.01×湿度×（0.99×気温－14.3）＋46.3〉。同じ気温でも**湿度**が高いほうがその値は高くなるというワケ。

　不快の度合いを表す**言葉**も決まっている。不快指数75以上で「やや暑い」、80以上で「暑くて汗が出る」、85以上で「暑くてたまらない」など、55以上で「**肌寒い**」だから数字の幅は狭い。

　ところで「不快の度合い」は人それぞれ。数値にはどれくらいの**信憑性**（しんぴょうせい）があるのか。

　全国のメディアに気象情報を提供している日本気象協会はこう説明する。

　「不快指数は蒸し暑さの目安として昔から採用しています。ただ、気温と湿度だけで計算していて、風や日照を**考慮に入れ**ていないので、場所によって不快感は違ってきます」

　風が1メートル吹くと**体感温度**は1度下がるといわれる。扇風機程度の風があれば、不快指数は10以上も下がったように感じられるそうだ。

　実はこの不快指数、もともとは1959年にアメリカの気象局が「冷房設定の目安」として開発したもの。室内のエアコンディションを適正に保つためのものだから、屋外ではあまり意味がない。

But the "discomfort index" actually has a long-established formula, namely: $0.81T + 0.01H (0.99T - 14.3) + 46.3$, where T = temperature and H = humidity. Even at the same temperature, higher **humidity** will yield a higher value.

There are also definitions for the **terminology** used to describe the level of "discomfort." An index value of 75 or higher is read as "rather hot," 80 or higher as "hot and sweaty," and 85 or higher as "unbearably hot" etc. The terminology is set in 5 point intervals, with 55 to 60 being "**chilly**."

However, the actually feeling of discomfort varies from person to person, so how much **credability** should we lend to the numbers?

"The discomfort index has a long history of use to measure heat and humidity. But as it doesn't **take into account** other factors such as wind or strength of sunlight, its results can often be different from the way the weather actually feels," the Meteorological Agency tells us. Even a breeze of 1 meter per hour can lower our **perception of the temperature** by a whole degree. Even the wind from an electric fan can make the discomfort index inaccurate by more than ten points.

Actually, the discomfort index is not a Japanese invention. It was first developed by the American Weather Bureau in 1959 as a guide for air-conditioner settings. But since it was developed to help regulate indoor conditions, it tends to loose a lot of its accuracy ourdoors.

紙にはなぜAとBの2サイズがあるのか?

　コピー用紙にAとBの2種類のサイズがあるのはなぜ?

　紙のサイズの規格には「紙加工仕上げ**寸法**」と「原紙の寸法」の2種類があり、いずれも戦後にJIS規格として定められた。

　コピー用紙などのAとBの違いは「紙加工仕上げ寸法」によるもので、正式にはA列とB列。A列は**国際規格**で、ドイツの工業規格をそのまま採用している。一方のB列は、江戸時代の公用紙「美濃紙」を基にしている。それぞれの列を用いた紙を判という。

　『トコトンやさしい紙の本』(日刊工業新聞社)の著者・小宮英俊氏はこう言う。

　「戦前まで、官公庁などでは今のB判サイズが主流でしたが、戦後、国際交流が進むと国際規格のA判サイズが**重宝される**ようになり、1993年には行政文書の用紙すべてがA判に統一されました」

　いまでは行政文書やほとんどのビジネス書類がA判を使っている。

　A列、B列ともに0から10まである。A0の半分がA1、A1の半分がA2、A2の半分がA3、A3の半分が

社会システムのギモン ● Problems with the Social System

Why does paper come in A sizes and B sizes?

Paper comes in two types of sizes in Japan: A and B. But why? When it comes to paper sizes, there are two types of standards: "paper processing finishing **dimensions**" and "body paper dimesnsions," both of which were established in the JIS after the war.

The difference between the A and B sizes commonly used in photocopy machines, for example, is one of processing finishing dimensions, officially known as "A-series" and "B-series." The A-series is the **international standard**, actually a direct copy of German industrial standards. The B-series, on the other hand, is based on the "*mino* paper" used by government during the Edo period.

Hidetoshi Komiya, author of *Paper Made Easy*, published by the Nikkan Kogyo Shimbun says: "Before the war, government used B sizes for almost all official business; but after the war, with the development of international exchange, the A sizes began to **catch on**. In 1993, A sizes were made official for all government business." Businesses as well use the A sizes now almost exclusively.

Sizes in the A-series and B-series are designated by numbers from 0 through 10, with each number representing a half-

A4と続く。Bも同様だが、通常使われているのは5か6までのサイズだ。

　A判は行政文書やビジネス文書、月刊誌、書籍、文庫など。B判は封筒や週刊誌、チラシなど、主に**日常的な用途**に使われている。
　このように国際規格と国独自の規格、2種類の紙のサイズを使い分けているのは世界的にも珍しいそうだ。
　ちなみに「原紙の寸法」は、製本や紙加工を行うために必要な**断裁余白**を含めた製紙業用の規格で、われわれ一般消費者にはほとんどなじみがない。

　ところで、近年ペーパーレス化が叫ばれているが、紙がなくなることはあるのだろうか。

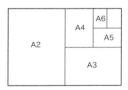

A1　594mm×841mm

B1　728mm×1030mm

　「電子メディアに比べ、紙は記録も簡単、閲覧もしやすく、保存性にも優れています。リサイクルなどの面でも、ますます紙の重要性が高まっています」（小宮氏＝前出）
　もっとも、オジサン世代は"髪"の存亡のほうが気になるのではあるが……。

size of the preceding number. So A3 is half the size of A2, A4 is half the size of A3, etc. B sizes are also derived in the same way, but B5 and B6 are the only sizes very commonly used.

A sizes are used for administrative and business documents, books, and monthly publications. B sizes are used for envelopes, weekly magazines, **flyers**, and other mainly **day-to-day applications**. Japan is unique in using both one international standard and one domestic standard for paper sizes at the same time.

And as for the "body paper dimension" standards, these are technical regulations used by the paper industry, including, for example, the **edge trimming margins** required for book making and paper processing, which seem to be well over the heads of us general consumers.

One more question for Mr. Komiya: "We hear so much about doing things 'paperless' these days. Is paper ever going to disappear?"

Answer: "Compared with electronic media, paper is easy to record on, easy to view, and is by no means devoid of its own merits when it comes to storage. Also as recycling becomes more advanced, paper is becoming more and more important."

That's good to know. On a lighter note, the Japanese words for "paper" and "hair" are homophones—both being pronounced *kami*. And among Japan's aging (and not unfrequently balding) workforce, all this talk of doing things "paperless" can lead to some rather unhumorous puns.

歩道をふさいで商品の搬入。警察は許可してるのか？

郊外の駅近くのショッピングセンターで、毎朝歩道をふさぐようにして商品の**搬入**が行われている。**通行**のじゃまだし、警察は許可しているのだろうか。

記者が目撃した場所は郊外の私鉄の駅から5分ほどの交差点の角にあるショッピングセンター。スーパーや100円ショップなどが入っているが、毎朝片側1車線の道路（しかも信号のある交差点から10メートルも離れていない）にトラックを止め、歩道をふさぐようにして商品を搬入しているのだ。

しかも、通行人がいてもあいさつの一つもなく「じゃまだ」というような態度を見せる業者さえいる。

大手スーパーの知人に聞いた。

「歩道を横切って商品を搬入しなければならないなんていう店の出店が許可されることはまずありませんよ」

と言ったが、現実に搬入していると伝えると、「信じられませんが、それが本当だとするとよほどの有力者に口を利いてもらったということでしょう」。

地元の"**センセイ**"を通じて警察に話をつけたのではないか、というのである。

社会システムのギモン ● Problems with the Social System

Is it legal for delivery trucks to park on the sidewalk while making their deliveries?

In suburban shopping districts, near the train station, every morning we see trucks parked half-way up on the sidewalks **making deliveries** to the shops. Do the police approve of this disturbance to **pedestrians** and traffic?

We came across one case five minutes from a private rail station in the suburbs. There's an intersection with a shopping center housing a supermarket, ¥100 shop, etc. Every morning, trucks pull up and park, blocking the sidewalk of the two-lane road—mind you, this is no more than 10 meters from the intersection—to make their deliveries to the shops. The drivers seem to pay no attention to people who are trying to walk by, and some of them even seem disgruntled with the pedestrians for getting in their way.

But here's what an acquaintance of ours connected with the supermarket industry had to say: "First of all, there's no way they would ever let a shop into the shopping center that would need to block the sidewalk for deliveries." But when we proceeded to tell him that they actually are blocking the sidewalk to make, he replied, "That's pretty hard to believe! They must have friends in pretty high places!" Which means, some **big-shot** must have gone and talked with the police for them.

そこで記者は地元の警察署の交通課に問い合わせてみた。○○交差点のショッピングセンターのことで、と記者が言うと、どうも苦情は少なくない様子で、
　「あれですか。指導しているんですけどね」と迷惑そうに答えた。
　「だって、あそこは信号のすぐそばですよ。車止めていいの?」
　「駐車じゃなくて、**停車**ですから」
　などと相手を弁護するような言葉も。
　「だけど、信号の近くにトラックを止めて荷物を店に搬入しても"停車"なんですか?」
　と記者が言うと今度はダンマリ。
　「ショッピングセンターから付け届けをもらって**目こぼし**してるんじゃないかと近隣の商店の人は言ってますよ」
　と記者は追及した。
　「そんなことは絶対にありません。何度も注意しているんですから」
　と警察は答える。
　しかし、先のスーパーの知人によれば、「一般の人から警察に**苦情**が入ると警察から連絡があるので、**ビール券**でも持って警察に謝りにいくのが普通」
　とのこと。記者は警察に苦情を言ったので、警察に届くビール券が増えたってことなのか?

社会システムのギモン ● Problems with the Social System

We tried asking the traffic division of the local police department. When we told them about the situation at this shopping center, the officer replied, "Yes, we're aware of the situation . . . We've instructed them about this in the past already," as though we were wasting his time.

"But it's right in front of the traffic signal," we continued. "Is it OK to park there?"

"They're not parking. They're just **stopping**," the officer replied, trying to defend them.

But he seemed at a loss for a good answer when we asked, "Can you really call that 'just stopping'? They're parking right in front of the traffic signal and getting out of their trucks to make their deliveries!" We continued: "People in the neighboring shops are saying that the shopping center must be paying the police off to **turn a blind eye to** things."

"That's absolutely false," the officer retorted. "We've warned them about this many times."

According to our friend connected with the supermarket industry, however, "If the police get a **complaint** from ordinary citizens, the police contact the shopping center, who in turn usually go to the police bearing gifts such as **beer coupons** to apologize." So our complaining to the police probably had little effect other than putting more beer in the police officer's belly.

通話料無料の110番。 誰が料金負担してるのか?

1度だけ110番に電話したことがある。交通事故を目撃し、最寄りの**公衆電話**からかけたのだ。

むろんタダだったが、カードやコインが必要だったとしてもかけたと思う。しかし電話回線を利用しているのは事実で、だれかがこのコストを負担しているはずだ。

NTT東日本に問い合わせてみた。「ああ、あれですか。課金しないシステムになっているのだと思います」(NTT東日本担当者)

つまり、通話しても料金がかからないようになっているということだ。

「法律で決まっているのですか?」と聞く。「調べてご返事します」と担当者は言い、翌日返事をしてくれた。「当社には**契約約款**というものがありまして、それに基づいたものです」と次のような「通話に関する料金の減免規定」について説明してくれた。

110、119、118などの緊急通報用の通話は減免の対象になっており、ほかにも地震などの災害が発生したときにNTTが指定した公衆電話から罹災者(りさい)がかける電話も対象になっている。言うまでもなくNTTはかつて「**公社**」だったので公共性のある通話には便宜を図(はか)っているということなのだろう。

社会システムのギモン ● Problems with the Social System

It's free to call the police on 1-1-0; but who actually foots the bill?

This writer has only had to call 1-1-0 once. I was witness to a traffic accident, and called from a nearby **payphone**. Of course, it's a toll-free call (but I think I would have called even if coins or a phone card were required). But since calling 1-1-0 does actually make use of the phone lines, there must be some costs involved. Who's paying?

The comment we got from a representative of Nippon Telegraph and Telephone (NTT) East Corporation was: "Ah, 1-1-0. I believe that's set up on a no-charge system." This means that their system doesn't record any costs generated by the call.

"Is it prescribed by law?" we asked.

"I'll have to check on that and get back to you," which he did the following day. "It's based on our company's **conditions of contract**," he said, and continued to explain about their "policy of reductions and exemptions of calling fees."

Emergency telephone numbers like 1-1-0, 1-1-9, and 1-1-8 are exempt from tolls charges. This policy also covers public phones which NTT designates for the victims of earthquakes and other disasters. Of course, NTT is a former **government-owned corporation**, and this policy reflects their effort to serve public calling needs.

さらに事情通がこう語る。

「電話は回線を引いたりと、システムをつくるときには膨大なコストがかかりますが、その後は一般回線から回収するだけ。**大してコストはかかりません。**公共性の高い通話をタダにしたところで、痛くもかゆくもないでしょう」

なるほど、そういうものなのか。

ちなみに故障の問い合わせなどNTTのサービスへの問い合わせも無料だが、「電報を打ちたいと思って104に番号を問い合わせたら規定の番号案内の料金を徴収された」と怒っている人がいた。

公共性の高い通話に便宜を図りながら、自社のサービスを案内するのに金を取っているのは**理不尽な気**が……。

あなたはかけたことありますか?
Ever had to call 1-1-0?

社会システムのギモン ● Problems with the Social System

Our well-informed NTT representative further explained that, "A huge amount of money is required to lay phone lines and build calling networks, but once all of that is in place, putting a call through is simply a matter of connecting the circuits and **costs virtually nothing**. So making these public service numbers toll free isn't costing anyone a dime."

As a side note, calls to request telephone repair or get information about NTT services are also toll-free. But we also heard from one disgruntled NTT customer: "I wanted to send a telegram and called 1-0-4 (directory assistance) to ask the number, but they still charged me the regular information fee."

Trying to serve public calling interests on the one hand, but then charging for information on their own company's services on the other, does seem a little **irrational**.

持ち主が現れない
忘れ物のカサはどうなるのか？

　梅雨時になると、電車の中にカサの忘れ物が目立つが、持ち主が引き取りにこなかったカサはどうなる？

　朝降っていた雨が帰りにはやんでいたり、「午後から雨」の予報が当たらなかったり……この時季、車内にカサを忘れてしまった経験はだれでも一度や二度はあるのではないだろうか。

　「電車の中の忘れ物で一番多いのがカサです。梅雨時などは、多い日で1日1000本以上。年間では何万本にもなりますね」（東京メトロ広報部）

　忘れ物のカサは、拾得された駅で1～2日保管された後、「遺失物集約駅」に集められ、そこで保管される（通常1週間程度）。

　「その間に落とし主からの**問い合わせがなかった**カサは、指定の警察署に届けます」（JR東日本広報）

　警察署で遺失物を受け取るには、駅で発行してもらった**証明書**などが必要だ。実際はわざわざ警察までカサを引き取りにくる人はまれで、約6カ月後には

社会システムのギモン ● Problems with the Social System

What happens to all those forgotten umbrellas?

You know the rainy season is really here when you start noticing abandoned umbrellas on the train. But if their owners never come to pick them up, what happens to them? During this time of the year, all of us have forgotten an umbrella on the train at least once or twice: the rain that that was falling when you left home in the morning may have stopped by the time you got to work, or that rain that the weather forecast said would start falling around midday may have just failed to show up.

According to the Tokyo Metro's press office, "Umbrellas are by far the most common of items passengers forget on trains. During rainy season, we may collect upwards of 1,000 umbrellas a day; over the course of a year, several tens of thousands."

Forgotten umbrellas are first kept at the station where they are found for 1 to 2 days, after which they are moved to a "lost item collection station" (usually for around a week). And according to JR East, "Umbrellas which are still **unclaimed** after that are handed over to the police."

If you're still interested in going to pick up your umbrella after it's made its way to the police station, you'll need to have a **certificate** issued by the train station. But it seems

鉄道会社にごっそり戻ってくるのだとか。
　民法と遺失物法の規定により、鉄道駅・車内での忘れ物は、持ち主が現れないと管理者である鉄道会社の**所有物**になる。

　引き取り手のないカサは、東京メトロの場合は「買い取り業者に一括して**引き渡し**」ている。JR東日本、JR長野など支社によっては、一部を毎年10月14日の「鉄道の日」前後に開催されるイベントでのチャリティーバザーに回すこともあるという。
　買い取り業者に渡ったカサは、さらにリサイクルショップなどの業者に卸される。中には1万円近くする高級ガサもあり、値段が安ければ中古でもそこそこ売れる商品なのだ。
　確かに、なくしがちなカサは**消耗品**と割り切ってしまえば、安く買うに越したことはない。

　客に**無料で配る**ためのカサをこのルートで安く仕入れる商売上手なレストランなどもあるというから、遺失物のカサは意外と活躍しているようだ。

that almost no one is this interested in getting their umbrella back. After six months, the umbrellas are once again returned to the train station. According to the **civil code** and the Lost Property Law, unclaimed items forgotten in trains or in stations become the **property** of the railway company.

In the case of the Tokyo Metro, these abandoned umbrellas are **handed over** in bulk to recycling agents. Some JR subsidiaries such as JR East and JR Nagano raffle them off at "Railway Day" charity bazaars each year on October 14.

The recycling agents further pass along some of the umbrellas to secondhand shops. Some of these forgotten umbrellas are actually expensive brand-name accessories originally costing as much as ¥10,000. Even used, they sell fairly well in the secondhand shops if the price is right. It doesn't seem strange either that if so many people treated umbrellas as though they were **disposable**, then when it comes time to buy one, why not get it as cheap as possible—secondhand.

Some restaurants even get in on the action and buy bundles of these umbrellas to **give away** to their customers who might be caught in the rain. You might forget about them the moment you step off the train, but these abandoned umbrellas have a rather interesting story of their own.

ゴミの分別方法はなぜ地域によって違う？

ゴミの分別収集。**ペットボトル**や紙パックに至るまで細かく分別収集するところもあれば、**可燃**と不燃を一緒くたにしてもOKなところも。なぜ地域によってバラバラなのか。

　家庭などから出る一般廃棄物（以後ゴミ）は、市町村単位で各自治体が責任を持って分別収集、廃棄処理することになっている。国の**指針**はあるが、それを受け入れて実施するかはそれぞれの**自治体**による。

　東京では、23区は「不燃」「可燃」「**資源**」の3分別収集が基本だが、可燃に廃食用油や古布を入れていい区とダメな区、不燃ゴミに乾電池を入れていい区とダメな区があるなど、細かな内訳は区によって異なる。

　各地域住民の生活レベルはさほど違わないはずなのに、これほどゴミの分別方法に違いが出てくるのには理由がある。

社会システムのギモン ● Problems with the Social System

Why do the garbage separation rules vary from area to area?

If you ever try throwing something away at a friend's house in another part of town, you may be surprised to find that the way they think about garbage is different from where you're from. In some areas residents have to go so far as to separate **plastic bottles** and milk cartons from ordinary recyclables, while in other areas, no distinction is even made between **combustible** and non-combustible garbage. Why the variation from region to region?

Each city, town, and village is responsible for its own garbage collection. The government does have **recommendations** on the way garbage should be collected, but whether those recommendations are followed or not is up to the individual **municipalities**.

The 23 wards of Tokyo all separate household garbage into three groups: "non-combustible," "combustible," and "**recyclable**." But is it OK to throw out used frying oil or old linens with the combustibles? In some wards, yes; in some wards, no. Is it OK to throw out used batteries with the non-combustibles? Again, it depends on the ward, with various definitions of what is OK for each group for each location. The way people live doesn't change so drastically from one area to another, but there is a reason why the garbage rules do?

東京では焼却施設や最終処分場の処理の違いもあるが、それぞれの自治体の**ゴミ分別**に対する意識や予算の違いによるところが大きい。細かく分別すればするほど中間処理などに費用がかかり、"かけたくても金がない"という自治体も出てくるという。ちなみに1991年の「資源利用促進法」以降、ビン、缶、**段ボール**はもとより、ペットボトル、紙パック、白色トレー、プラスチック容器、廃家電などがリサイクル対象品となっている。これだけの品目をすべてリサイクルしようとすれば、手間や金がかかるのは当然だ。

　一方で、川崎市では、現在、リサイクルの対象として分別収集している缶、ビン、ペットボトル、乾電池、小物金属以外は、**衛生的**処理と埋め立て地の延命化を図るため、「普通ごみ」として全量焼却処理している。

　たしかに、川崎市のようにリサイクル対象品以外、燃やせるものはすべて燃やしてしまったほうがいいような気もするが……。

　「そういう考え方もありますが、**ダイオキシン**の問題などもあり、全焼却は現実的ではありません」（ゴミ処理の関係者）

　現在のところ、東京都の不燃ゴミは、選別の後に埋め立てられている。みなさん、"**分別**（ふんべつ）"のある分別を。

社会システムのギモン ● Problems with the Social System

There are differences in the garbage treatment facilities available to Tokyo's different areas, but the differences in people's awareness of the importance of **garbage separation**, as well as the budget a locality is willing to allot to garbage treatment, are the biggest factors. The more groups garbage is separated into for recycling, the greater the processing costs; and many local governments find themselves in a position where they'd like to do more to recycle, but they just don't have the money. Still, the Recycling Promotion Act of 1991 specifies not only the usual bottles, cans, and **cardboard**, but also plastic bottles, milk cartons, Styrofoam trays, plastic containers, and electric appliances as garbage subject to recycling. For local governments, the cost of recycling all of these is naturally expensive.

The city of Kawasaki, however, looking for a **hygienic** and sustainable way of dealing with non-recyclables, currently burns all of its combustible garbage except of cans, glass and plastic bottles, batteries, and miscellaneous metals.

When you think of the costs involved with keeping a landfill, just burning all the combustibles doesn't seem like such a bad idea. But according to one garbage processing company we asked, "It sounds nice, but it really isn't practical. There's also the problem of **dioxin** emissions . . ."

And as for Tokyo, all of its non-combustibles are sorted, and then make their way to the landfill. And a word to our readers: it's alright to be **picky** when sorting your garbage.

国会図書館にエロ本はあるのか？

　国内外の書籍・雑誌が800万冊以上収められているという**国立国会図書館**。エロ本も置いてあるのだろうか。
　さっそく国会図書館広報に尋ねてみた。
　「成人向け雑誌もありますし、基本的にすべて閲覧できます」
　さすがは18歳以上しか入れない国会図書館だ。

　実際に館内で蔵書を検索してみると、アリス出版の自販機本「Chris（クリス）」が2冊ヒット。もちろん閲覧もできた。エロ本どころか、コンピューターのハッキング方法や**火炎瓶**の作り方を載せたサブカル雑誌まである。「国立国会図書館法では、国内の**出版物**はすべて国会図書館に納本しなければならず、違反すると過料を科せられることになっています。**自費出版**でも個人出版でも、不特定多数に配る目的の出版物のすべてが対象です」（広報）

　とはいえ実際に過料を取ったケースはなく、出版元が納本しなければ蔵書にはならない。合法エロ本

社会システムのギモン ● Problems with the Social System

Do they keep any dirty books at the National Diet Library?

The **National Diet Library** boasts a collection of over 8 million books and magazines, both from Japan and from overseas. But do they really have anything sleazy worth looking at?

We went straight to the NDL and asked.

"Yes, we do have adult magazines. And you're free to view any materials you like," we were delighted to hear... **Way to go**, National Diet Library! You even have to be 18 or over to get in.

A little search of their catalog turned up two numbers of "Chris," published by Alice Japan, typical smut you get out of vending machines. And, of course, we were able to view these materials. But the fun didn't stop with erotic periodicals. We also came across "sub-culture" mags explaining how to hack a network and how to make a **Molotov cocktail**. "According to the National Diet Library Act, Japanese publishers are required to submit copies of all their **publications** to the NDL, and we can fine any publisher who fails to do so. Even **in-house publications**, publications made by individuals, and publications for free distribution are subject to the law," the NDL informed us.

But we also learned that they've never actually fined anyone, and that the library only gets what publishers send of

も、すべてが収められているわけではないのだ。また、裁判で違法とされた出版物などは納本されても閲覧できない。

ちなみに国会図書館は2004年10月からシステムが変わった。**登録カード**を作れば、住所・氏名を毎回書かなくても入館できるようになり、午後4時までだった平日の閲覧請求が6時まで延長。使いやすくなったのはありがたいが、図書館側では「雑誌の**グラビア**などが破られないよう常に気を配らなければならない」（広報）のが悩みの種。

国家所蔵のエロ本はみんなのもの。持ち帰りは厳禁だぞ。

もともと18歳以上しか入館できないのだが……?
So that's why you have to be over 18 to get in ...

their own free will. So they don't actually have every legal racy magazine in Japan. And publications which have been deemed illegal by a court are not available to be viewed.

In 2004, the library changed its admissions system. Now, if you fill out a **registration card**, you don't have to write your name and address every time you want to go in. And the viewing hours, which used to finish at 4 PM, have been extended to six o'clock. We think it's great that the library has become easier to use, but their public relations office tells us that one of their biggest worries is "making sure there's no damage to or loss of the newest **gravure** idol magazines."

Remember, it may be smut, but at the National Diet Library, it's public property. Don't even think of taking it home!

同じ番地なのに
電柱の住所表示の色が違う?

　不慣れな町を歩くときに**重宝**する**電柱**の住所表示。ところが同じ町の同じ番地であるにもかかわらず、表示の色が違うものがある。何か理由があるのか?

　電柱に張られた広告の下側に表示される四角で囲まれた住所表示。次頁の写真の電柱は緑色になっているが、青色のものもよく見かける。

　実はこれ、青色がNTT東日本の電柱で緑色が東京電力の電柱なのだ。NTTの電信柱に掲示されている広告の住所表示は青色（一部灰色）で、東京電力の電柱に掲示されている住所表示は緑色というワケ。
　電柱広告の歴史は古く、明治23(1890)年に始まったという。現在は全国に広がって、電力系、NTT系それぞれに**下請け**の広告会社がある。

　関東圏では東京電力系で約60万件、NTT東日本系で約11万件の電柱広告があるそうだ。
　いずれも初回製作料1万2000円、月々の広告料1600～3000円となかなかリーズナブル。広告主は

社会システムのギモン ● Problems with the Social System

Why are the addresses on telephone poles displayed in different colors, even at the same address?

When you're trying to find your way in an unfamiliar part of town, the addresses displayed on **telephone poles** can be a **life-saver**. But even at the same address, there can be two address displays in different colors. Is there some reason for this?

The addresses are usually indicated in the rectangular area at the bottom of advertisements on the telephone poles. In the picture on the next page, the display is in green, but others are in blue.

It turns out that the poles with blue displays are the property of Nippon Telegraph and Telephone East Corporation; and the green ones, the property of the Tokyo Electric Power Company. (NTT East's are occasionally also found in grey.)

The history of advertising on poles used for telephone and power lines is an old one, going back to 1890. Nowadays, you can find these advertisements virtually anywhere in the country, and both the telephone companies and the electric companies have their own **dedicated** advertising agencies.

In the Kanto area, Tokyo Electric has 600,000 poles bearing advertisements; and NTT East's number 110,000.

Most businesses using this advertising are **pawn shops**, doctor's offices, small retailers, and the like—businesses

質店や病院、小売店など地域密着型の商業者が多く、中には50年以上も掲示し続けている広告主もいるという。

ちなみに電柱広告は唯一**公道**に掲示できる広告。個人でも広告主になれるが、不特定多数の人間のための誘導案内(例えば"○○質店この道を曲がってスグ"のような)などに限られるため、「花嫁募集」などという"極私的"広告は出すことができない。

そうした公共性の高さから、住所表示も公共サービスの意味合いが強く、町名のほかに**通学路、避難経路**なども一部では表示されている。

さりげなく町の役に立っている電柱広告。一度、目を凝らしながら町を歩いてみては?

緑色はNTTの電柱、青色が東京電力の電柱

Green for phone poles, blue for electric.

with their roots firmly planted locally. The advertisements cost a ¥12,000 initial set-up fee, and the monthly costs are reasonable: from ¥1,600 to ¥3,000 per month. Some of these accounts have been using the same advertisement for as long as 50 years.

Telephone pole advertisements are the only form of advertisement allowed on **public roads**. The owner of the advertisement can be a private individual, but the content is restricted to business names and directions for how to get there (like "Acme Pawn Shop, Turn Next Corner.") "Private" advertisements, such as "Bride Wanted," are not allowed.

And being "public" advertisements, the display of the address of the pole's location can also be considered a form of public service. Many of the poles also indicate **school zones** and **emergency evacuation routes**.

So these advertisements are just another example of the utilities companies always at your service. Try checking them out next time you're walking around your own part of town.

降水確率はどうやって決めている？

天気予報で気になるのが降水確率の数字。降水確率の「％」はどうやって決めているのだろう？

「**降水確率**は、さまざまなデータから総合的に判断しています。**気圧配置**だけでなく、全国の**気象台**から送られてくるデータなど、風や気温などの時間変化をスーパーコンピューターで計算して、はじき出します。物理学の方程式を使った数値予報です」（気象庁）

計算方法は、簡単に言うとこうだ。
過去に同じような気象条件の日が100回あったとする。そのうち70回雨が降っていたら、降水確率は70％になる。73％などの半端な数字が出てきたら**四捨五入**。表示は10％きざみだ。

また、これは「予報区内で**一定の時間内**に1ミリ以上の雨または雪が降る確率」で、「**降水量**」は関係ない。30％より90％のほうが大降りのように感じるが、少量の雨がパラパラでも降る可能性が高くなるだけだ。

社会システムのギモン ● Problems with the Social System

How is the "chance of precipitation" calculated?

What everybody wants to know when they watch the news report in the morning is: "What's the chance of rain today?" But how do they calculate this percentage?

According to the National Meteorological Agency, "The **chance of precipitation** is decided based on a wide range of collected data. Data including wind speed and temperature are collected from **meteorological stations** all over the country, and the differences in these data over time are evaluated in conjunction with **atmospheric pressure distributions** using a supercomputer to derive the final percentages."

The method of calculation, stated simply, is as follows: Let's say there are 100 days on record with meteorological conditions similar to today's. If it rained on 70 of those days, then today's chance of rain is 70%, with percentages **rounded** to the nearest 10%.

Furthermore, this percentage represents the chance of "rainfall or snowfall in excess of 1 mm **over a given period of time** for the given location," and has nothing to do with the "**amount of rainfall**." So while 90% might sound like a downpour and 30% like a light sprinkle, this is not the case. The rain on a 90% day may be just a light sprinkle, but it is more likely to fall.

ところで、快晴の日など、「降水確率0％」はよく見るが、「降水確率100％」は見かけない。
　なぜなのか？
　「たしかに、100％という予報はほとんどありません。昭和55（1980）年に降水確率を発表して以来、数えるほどしかないはずです。正確なデータが残っていないためうろ覚えですが、最近では6、7年前の梅雨時期に1度あったきり（2004年6月現在）。6時間に1ミリ以上の雨が降る割合は20％であり、**予報**に含まれている不確実さを考えると、発生頻度の比較的少ない現象を100％と予想する回数は少なくなります」（気象庁）

　100％と予想される回数は少ないということか。どうりで、すでに雨が降っているのに「降水確率60％」なんて予報が出されることもあるわけだ。
　ちなみに、梅の花が咲くのは通常2月ごろなのに、なぜ「梅雨」と書くのかというと、これは花ではなく実。梅の実が**熟す**時期にあたるから「梅雨」なのだ。

社会システムのギモン ● Problems with the Social System

On days without a cloud in the sky, you may sometimes see a 0% chance of rain on the news, but you never see 100%. Why not?

A representative from the NMA (speaking in June 2004) told us: "Indeed, a forecast of 100% is very rare, with only a handful of instances since we began forecasting the chance of precipitation in 1980. Offhand, I can only remember one instance six or seven years ago during the rainy season. In actuality, the average chance of rainfall over any 6 hour period is only 20% in Japan. So when you consider the inherent factor of error that goes along with **weather forecasting**, it makes it hard to make a forecast of 100% for something that may never actually happen."

On the other hand, on days when it's already raining you might see forecasted "60% chance of rain." Maybe they should have a little more faith in their data.

And as for the rainy season, even though it comes every summer, why is it called *tsuyu* (written with the *kanji* for "plum" and "rain") when the plum trees bloom in February? Actually, this is a reference to the fruit, not the flowers. The rainy season coincides with the time each year when the plums themselves **ripen**.

紙幣の視覚障害者用「点字マーク」が消えた!?

2004年に発行された新紙幣。よく見ると旧紙幣にあった**点字タイプ**の視覚障害者用識別マークがなくなっている。これはどうしたことか？

旧紙幣は、裏面右下に点字タイプの"すかし"の識別マークがあった。ドーナツ状の「凹（くぼ）み」が1000円札は1つ、5000円札は縦に2つ、1万円札は横に2つ。どうしてなくなってしまったのか？ 日本銀行に尋ねてみた。

「識別マークがなくなったわけではありません。新紙幣は表側の左右下に凸状の記号が印刷されています。**深凹版印刷**（ふかおうはん）という最新の技術を使った識別マークを導入しています」（日本銀行政策広報）

言われてみれば、1万円札にはL字形、5000円札には八角形、1000円札には横一文字の記号が印刷されている。これが新しい視覚障害者用識別マークだ。深凹版印刷は、従来の"すかし"よりもザラつきがあり、指で触ったときに判別しやすいのだという。さらに5000円と1万円の**高額紙幣**には表面がツルツ

What? No more denomination indicators for the blind on the new yen bills!?

New yen bills were introduced in 2004, and if you haven't noticed, it seems that the **braille-like type** used for the blind to distinguish between denominations has disappeared. What's happened?

The old bills bore braille-like "**watermarks**" in the lower right of the reverse of the bills. A doughnut shaped **indentation** was used to indicate ¥1,000; two of these indentations were arranged vertically for ¥5,000 bills; and two doughnuts aligned horizontally indicated a ¥10,000 bill. But why have these been done away with in the new bills? Here's what the Bank of Japan had to say.

"Denomination indicators haven't been done away with at all. The new bills have elevated indicators printed on the bottom left and right of the face of the bill. The latest technology, known as '**deep-engraving printing**,' was introduced for the new indicators."

So upon closed examination, we found an L-shaped elevation on ¥10,000 bills, two bars arranged in an upside-down V on ¥5,000 bills, and a single vertical bar on ¥1,000 bills. The elevations made by deep-engraving printing are rougher than, and easier to distinguish by touch, than the old watermark-type indicators. ¥5,000 and ¥10,000 bills also now

ルしたホログラムも付いているので、これも判別材料になりそうだ。

　とはいえ、これだけ大幅に識別マークを一新すると、かえって混乱してしまうのではないか？　普段からなじみのある点字タイプのほうがわかりやすいのでは？　視覚障害者向けに識別マーク変更のアナウンスはしているのか？　しつこく質問したところ、旧来のマークも「あくまでデザインで点字ではない」そうで、デザイン上のことは財務省に聞いてくれと言われてしまった。

　「深凹版印刷による識別マークの導入にあたっては、サンプルを日本盲人会連合などに**モニタリング**してもらい、すかしよりも判別しやすいとの意見が出ました。ただ、視覚障害者に向けて、マーク変更のアナウンスを特別にしたことはありません。一般の報道発表のみです」（財務省理財局）

　最新技術を盛り込んだ新紙幣も、「バリアフリー」にはほど遠い？

新しい識別マークは最新の技術
New indicators incorporate the latest printing technology.

bear smooth holograms which can also help to differentiate these **high-denomination bills**.

But by changing the denomination indicators, mightn't they actually be making things harder on the blind? One would think they would be more comfortable with the old indicators they were used to. Did they make any announcement of the new indicators to the blind community? Perhaps the Bank of Japan got fed up with all our questions, but in the end their answer was, "It's not braille anyhow. It's just a design," and referred us to the Ministry of Finance if we had any questions about the design.

"Before introducing the new deep-engraving printed indicators, we sent samples to the Japan Federation of the Blind for **evaluation**. They found that the new indicators are actually easier to use than the old watermarks. But there wasn't any announcement of the new bills specifically targeted at the blind, only the usual press releases," the Ministry of Finance told us.

Even with the latest technology, it seems we still have a way to go before the government really makes money "barrier-free."

なぜ水道料金だけ
2ヵ月ごとの請求なのか？

電気やガスの料金は1カ月ごとに徴収されるのに、なぜ**水道料金**だけは2カ月まとめて請求されるのか？

「水道メーターの**検針**が2カ月に1度と決まっているので、それに合わせて隔月で請求させていただいております」と言うのは、東京都水道局。それなら、毎月検針すれば済む話ではないのか？

「そうしたいのはやまやまなのですが、経費の問題があり、毎月検針にすると、人件費などが現在の1.7倍になるという**試算**が出ています。徴収額を知らせる通信費も倍かかるわけで、その分を水道料金に上乗せすることになるので、おいそれとはいかないんですよ。申し訳ありません」（同サービス推進部）

恐縮した様子で謝られ、思わず「文句ではないし、料金が上がるのは困るので今のままでいいですよ」と答えてしまった。

実は、以前は6カ月に1度の検針しか行っていなかったそうで、半年間の3回の請求のうち最初の2回は、過去の実績から推定した使用量を徴収。検針で使用水量が確定する3回目に、差額を精算する形式だっ

社会システムのギモン ● Problems with the Social System

Why does the water bill only come once every two months?

The electric and gas companies charge for their services every month. So why does the **water bill** only come every other month?

"The main reason is that we only send people out to **read the meters** once every other month, so we schedule our billing accordingly," was the answer given by the Tokyo Metropolitan Government Bureau of Waterworks. So, wouldn't sending people out to read the meters once a month do the trick?

"We'd love to be able to do that, but it isn't as easy as it sounds," their service department told us. Our **estimates** show that reading the meters once a month would push our personnel costs up 70%, and monthly billing would double what we spend in postal fees . . . so we're sorry we can only bill on a bimonthly basis for the time being."

We weren't expecting to get an apology. "We're not complaining," we told them. "Nobody wants water fees to go up, so please keep things just the way they are."

In the past, however, they used to read the meters only twice a year, and of the three bills sent out over the six-month period, the first two were estimates of actual water usage based on the previous meter reading. After the next meter

た。この6カ月検針では、月ごとの使用水量に差があると、料金精算時に**利用者**の**負担**が大きくなってしまう場合（料金の波うち）があるため、4カ月検針に移行。さらに1995年から**2カ月ごとの検針**になったという経緯だ。

「生活サイクル上、ほかの公共料金と同様に毎月徴収にしてもらいたいという声も多く寄せられており、2004年1月の**中期事業指針**で、毎月徴収実施を発表して**検討段階**に入っていますが、現在のところお客さまへのサービスの点やシステム開発の費用の問題などもあり、結論が出ない状況にあります」（同営業部）

毎月徴収になった場合も、当面は人件費などの問題により隔月検針。以前のように最初の月は推定使用量分が請求され、翌月に**差額を調整**するかたちになりそうだという。

だったら今のまま隔月徴収でいいんじゃないの？

reading, the actual amount of water used would be calculated and a third adjustment bill sent out to collect what still remained to be paid. If the amount of water a person uses varies throughout the year, this billing system can place a heavy **burden** on the **consumer** when an enormous bill comes, and this system was eventually replaced with meter readings once every four months. **Bimonthly readings** were introduced in 1995.

Their sales department informed us: "We often hear from consumers that it would be more convenient to be billed every month, just like the other bills they have to pay; and in our **mid-term policy directives** issued in 2004, we announced the introduction of monthly billing, and are currently in the **planning stages**. But due to concerns over customer service and development costs for a monthly billing system, we still can't say for sure when it's going to happen."

But even if they do switch to monthly billing, actual readings will still be bimonthly to keep personnel costs down. Like in the old days, one month's bill will be an estimate of water usage based on the previous month's reading, with the next month's bill being an **adjustment**.

In that case, why not just leave the bimonthly billing as it is?

再生紙は何回くらい"再生"されるのか?

　再生紙で作られた新聞や雑誌は、また再生紙の**材料**として回収されていく。紙は、いったい何回くらい再生できるものなのだろうか。

　「紙の再生は、3～5回が限界といわれています。再生を繰り返すうちに**繊維**の表面のシワがすり減って、繊維そのものが細かくなっていく。ついには、紙として再結合することができなくなるんです」(日本製紙連合会)

　再生紙は、古紙や新しいパルプを水に溶いてブレンドして作る。劣化が進んだ古紙の割合が多くなるにつれて、できあがる再生紙の質も下がる。おおむね、①OA紙②新聞③雑誌④段ボールの順だ。それぞれの再生過程で、劣化しきった古紙の繊維は、印字のインクなどの**不純物**と一緒に除去され、焼却されてしまう。

　「古紙が家具や**断熱材**として再生されることもあります。この場合も、捨てられれば、やはり焼却処分ですね」(同連合会＝前出)

　一方、再生紙で作られたイスや机もあるし、**棺桶**なんてものもあるんだとか。古紙の再生方法はいろいろあるが、結局のところ、最後は燃やされてしまうのだ。

社会システムのギモン ● Problems with the Social System

How many times is recycled paper actually "recycled"?

Magazines and newspaper made from **recycled paper** are collected again as **materials** to be recycled. How many times can paper be actually recycled?

"The recycling limit of paper is said to be three to five times. When recycled repeatedly, the grain of the paper **fiber** becomes gradually worn out and flat, and the fibers themselves shrink. Eventually, they won't be able to bond together as paper anymore," says the Japan Paper Industry Union.

Recycled paper is made by dissolving used paper and new pulp into water. As the amount of old paper blended in paper production increases, the quality of recycled paper decreases. The order of paper quality is, generally, (1) printing paper, (2) newspaper, (3) magazine paper, and (4) cardboard. During each recycling procedure, worn out fibers are removed as **impurities**, along with the printed ink, and burned up.

"Old paper can also be used as **insulation** or furniture material. In this case, when it is thrown away, it is incinerated," the Japan Paper Industry Union adds.

In addition, besides chairs and tables, there are even **coffins** made from recycled paper. So there may be several ways to recycle paper, but in the end, it's all destined to be burned up.

Part 2

街中のギモン
Problems in the Town

皇居の周りを走るジョギングはなぜ左回り?

皇居の周りをジョギングするサラリーマンやOL。その様子を眺めていて「おやっ」と気付いたことがある。みな時計の針とは逆=左回りで走っているのだ。右回りの人はごくまれ。ルールでもあるのだろうか。

そういえば陸上のトラック競技も左回り。スピードスケート、野球のベースもそうだ。やはりジョギングと左回りには因果関係があるのでは? ところがスポーツ科学の専門家はこう言う。

「**たまたまですよ**。陸上競技のトラックが左回りというのも、最初にそう決められたから。その理由を知るには、古代のスポーツ史にまでさかのぼらなきゃならない」(某スポーツ科学研究所)

暗礁に乗り上げたかにみえた"左回り"の疑問だが、ナゾを解くカギは意外なところにあった。カギを与えてくれたのは早稲田大学理工学部教授の渡辺仁史氏。「建築」の専門家である。

「人間とはそもそも左回りで歩く生き物なんです」と言う渡辺教授の理論をまとめると、
①人間は右利き左利きにかかわらず右足が長い。その

街中のギモン ● Problems in the Town

Why does everyone jog around the Imperial Palace counterclockwise?

There's something you may notice if you have a look at the business men and office workers jogging around the Kokyo, the **Imperial Palace** of Japan: everyone runs **counterclockwise**. You'll hardly ever see anyone running in the opposite direction. Is it some kind of rule?

But come to think of it, all track events run their courses counterclockwise. Speed skating is the same; the order of the bases in baseball, too. So is there some kind of **causal relationship** between jogging and going counterclockwise? Here's the answer we got from an expert in sport sciences.

"It's just a **coincidence**. Even for track-and-field events, running counterclockwise is just a matter of convention. To try to find some kind of reason behind it, you'd have to go back and try to examine the ancient history of sports."

But right when we were ready to give up on finding any answer to the mystery of running counterclockwise, we got an unexpected clue from out of the blue. The **clue** was given to us by Professor Hitoshi Watanabe, a specialist in construction, of the Faculty of Science and Engineering at Waseda University.

"Moving to the left and walking in a counterclockwise direction are inherent parts of human nature," he tells us. To summarize Professor Watanabe's theory: (1) Regardless

ため目隠しで歩いても左にそれやすい
②大部分の人の利き足は右。よって右足で蹴る力が強く、左回りのほうが楽
③心臓は左にあり、それをかばうために左側を歩く習性がある
④かつての武士が刀を差していたのは左。すれ違ったときツバがぶつからないように左側通行が習慣になった――等々。

　渡辺教授は長年の**実験**と**検証**によってこの理論を導き出した。ちなみに遊園地でも７割の客が左回りで園内を巡るそうな。

　「当然、この"左回りの法則"は建築にも有効です。**非常通路**や**階段**も左回りにしたほうが、いざという時逃げやすいのです」（渡辺教授＝前出）

　人間の不思議な**習性**。まさに目からウロコである。

"左回りの法則"は人間の習性だった！
Running counterclockwise: human instinct or mere coincidence?

of whether a person is right- or left-handed, the right leg is longer than the left. That's why it's easy for people to drift to the left when walking **blindfolded**. (2) Most people are "right-footed," thus having more strength to "kick" with the right leg. This makes running counterclockwise feel more natural. (3) Humans instinctively walk on the left, to protect the heart which is in the left side of the body. (4) Samurai and swordsmen used to wear their swords on their left hips. This made passing on the left customary to prevent two samurai's swords from touching each other, and to prevent the fight that could ensue . . . etc. etc. Professor Watanabe has spent years of **experimentation** and **investigation** building up his theory. He's even found that 70% of visitors to amusement parks make their way around the grounds progressing counterclockwise.

You wonder what any of this might have to do with his "specialty," construction? "It's safest to build **emergency passages** and **staircases** so that people can move in a counterclockwise direction. During an emergency, it's better if people can move in the way that's most natural for them," he says.

Who would have thought that something like running counterclockwise could be an expression of human **instinct**!

神社にはなぜ
玉砂利が敷かれているの？

歩くたびにシャリシャリと鳴る玉砂利。心地よく、情緒があるが、**神社**の参道や境内に玉砂利が敷かれているのはなぜなのか？

日本を代表する神社のひとつ明治神宮は、細かい**玉砂利**が境内一面に敷き詰められている。

「そもそも玉砂利の玉とは魂や御霊と同じで、霊的なものが宿ると考えられていました。また、"玉のような赤ん坊"というように、"美しい""大切"という**意味**もある。つまり御霊のこもった大切な石という意味があるのです」（明治神宮総務課）

玉砂利を踏みしめるときに鳴る音にも意味があるという。

「柏手や本殿前の鈴と同様に、あの澄んだ音は身と心を**清める**ためのもの。また、雨が降っても参拝者の着物のすそが汚れないように石を敷き詰めたという実用的な理由も昔はあったようです」（同総務課）

街中のギモン ● Problems in the Town

Why do so many Shinto shrines use pea gravel to pave their grounds?

There's something comforting and sentimental about the sound of the pebbles crunching together as you walk through a **Shinto shrine**, but why do so many shrines use loose gravel like this to pave their grounds?

One of Japan's most representative Shinto shrines, Meiji Shrine, uses **pea gravel** to pave its entire courtyard.

"Originally, the *tama* in *tama-jari*, just as in the words *tamashii* (spirit) and *mitama* (departed soul), represented the belief in a spiritual property of that thing. Also, as we say in Japanese 'a baby as sweet as *tama*,' the word has **connotations** of 'beautiful' and 'precious.' So we can take the word *tama-jari* to mean 'precious stones filled with the spirit of the departed souls.'"

There's also meaning to the sound the pebbles make as you walk on them.

"Just like the sound of the clapping of hands and the bells before the main sanctuary, the sound of the pea gravel is something to **purify** the body and mind. There's also a practical reason for using gravel to pave the grounds: so that even on rainy days, the hems of worshipers' kimonos won't get muddy." (Answers by Meiji Shrine's administration department)

一方、**世界遺産**に登録された日光東照宮(にっこうとうしょうぐう)の境内は、こぶし大の玉砂利がゴロゴロしている。これは鬼怒川の支流で取れる**油分の多い石**で、「栗石(くりいし)」と呼ばれるもの。

　「日光では年間の3分の2近く雨が降りますが、**湿気(しっけ)**は漆(うるし)を多く使った建物の大敵。油分の多い栗石を敷き詰めることで湿気を防ぎます。江戸時代の宮大工の知恵が今でも生きているのです」(東照宮総務課)

　土地柄(がら)によって玉砂利にもさまざまな工夫がなされているのだ。では、首相の**公式参拝**をめぐって毎年注目を浴びている靖国神社(やすくにじんじゃ)はどうか？ 問い合わせると、こんな答えが……。

　「お年寄りの**参拝者**から歩きにくいという声が上がり、2000年から2004年にかけて順次玉砂利を撤去しました」

　退役軍人など年配者の参拝が多いことで知られる靖国ならではのエピソードだ。

　庭や玄関に玉砂利を敷いた個人宅もある。見た目もさることながら、踏みしめたときに音が鳴ることから防犯にも役立つそうだ。

豊川稲荷の境内
A view of the grounds of Toyokawa Inari Shrine.

On the other hand, at Nikko Tosho-gu, a registered UNESCO **World Heritage Site**, they have gravel as big as your fist strewn across the grounds. This cobble, called *kuri-ishi*, is taken from the tributaries of the river Kinu-gawa and has a **high oil content**.

"In Nikko, it rains almost two out of three days of the year, and **humidity** is the greatest enemy of highly lacquered buildings like we have here. But we can control the humidity by using *kuri-ishi* with their high oil content to pave the grounds. This is an example of the wisdom of the old temple and shrine builders that is still being put to use today." (Answer by Tosho-gu's administration department)

So we can see that a lot of thought goes into deciding which kind of gravel will be best for a particular location. Well then, how about Yasukuni Shrine, which manages to find its way into the international spotlight every year over the controversy surrounding the Prime Minister's **official visits**? Here's what they had to say about gravel: "So many of our older **worshipers** complained of it being difficult to walk on, so from 2000 to 2004 we gradually phased out all the gravel paving"; not too hard to imagine when you think of the age of Japan's WWII veterans, one of the main groups of Yasukuni's faithful.

On a lighter note, there are also those who have chosen pea gravel to pave their gardens and the areas around their homes. More importantly than what it looks like, the sound it makes is sure to keep the burglars away.

お札の肖像画は誰が描いている?

紙幣の印刷は、現在独立行政法人の国立印刷局がを行っている。

「**お札の肖像画**は、工芸官という専門の技術者が描いています。まず、残された肖像画や彫像をもとに、筆と絵の具で**原図**をおこす工芸官がいます。さらにそれを、高度な技術を持った熟練の工芸官が彫刻し、原版を作製するのです」(国立印刷局広報室)

工芸官は、れっきとした国家公務員。一般の職員とは別枠で「工芸官」として採用される。美大や芸大の出身者が多いが、中には高卒者もいるという。

「現在、工芸官は約30人。ふだんは**国債**や切手などのデザインをしています。いわば"公務員デザイナー"ですね」(同広報室)

ところで、紙幣に人物が描かれるのには理由があ

街中のギモン ● Problems in the Town

Who draws the portraits printed on our money?

It's actually the National Printing Bureau (one of the Independent Administrative Institutions) which is now responsible for printing money.

"The portraits to be used for **bank notes** are drawn by expert artists known as *kogei-kan*. Firstly, there are the *kogei-kan* who make a **draft portrait** of the subject with brush and paint based on an existing sculpture or picture. Then, a veteran *kogei-kan* engraves the plate from which the printing is done, based on the draft portrait." (Answer by the National Printing Bureau's press office)

Kogei-kan are very elite civil servants, and they are hired through a completely separate process from other government employees. They are usually graduates of prestigious fine arts academies, but there are a few who are only high school graduates.

"Currently there are only around 30 *kogei-kan*. When they aren't working on new currency, their everyday work usually consists of making designs for **government bonds** and postage stamps. You can think of them as kind of like the graphic designers of the government," says the National Printing Bureau's press office.

As a side note, there's a reason for using portraits in the

る。人物像は建築物などに比べて模刻、模写が難しいうえ、人の顔は印象に残りやすいため、わずかな違いでも容易に判別できるからだ。

紙幣刷新の大きな目的は**偽造**防止。2004年の刷新の背景には、大量の偽札が出回ったことがあった。偽造防止には、こまめにデザインを一新することが有効なのだ。新紙幣には、見る角度によって像が変わる「ホログラム」や、棒状の模様を透かしで入れた「すき入れバーパターン」といった最新技術も盛り込まれている。

2004年の日本銀行券の大幅な**刷新**は20年ぶりのことだったが、世界的に紙幣の刷新サイクルは短くなっている。それだけ偽造技術も向上しているということか。

"公務員デザイナー"がいた!
The handiwork of a "government graphic designer."

design of bank notes. Compared with images of buildings, for example, a portrait is harder to engrave or duplicate. Also, the expression of the subject's face makes a lasting impression on our minds, making it easy to notice even slight differences.

The whole reason for making new currency in the first place is to prevent **counterfeiting**. A big motivation for the decision to redesign Japan's currency in 2004 was the large volume of counterfeit bills in circulation at that time. Taking great pains to make a good design is an effective counter-measure against counterfeiting. The new bills have been designed using the latest technology, including holograms and watermarked bar patterns.

The year 2004 marked the first big **renovation** for Bank of Japan notes in 20 years, but on a global scale, the time frame in which new currency needs to be designed keeps getting shorter and shorter. It just goes to show that no matter how much technology progresses, the counterfeiters just keep getting cleverer.

露出過剰は
どこまで見せたら罪になる？

夏は、ギャルたちが身も心も開放的になる季節。

それにしても近ごろのギャルの服装は開放的すぎやしないか。見せブラ、見せパンなどという「**見せる下着**」がはやっているというし、中には肌の露出も半乳、半尻は当たり前なんてギャルもいるから目のヤリ場に困る。もちろん全裸で街を歩けば立派な**公然わいせつ罪**だが、こうした**露出ギャル**、捕まることはないのだろうか。警察庁広報室に聞いてみた。

「全裸で街を歩くストリーキングならともかくファッションでしょ？　捕まったなんて話、聞いたことありませんよ。どこまで見せたらダメという線引きもありませんし、公然わいせつ罪の適用は難しいでしょうね」

あっけなく無罪放免だが、そもそも"わいせつ"とは何か。

街中のギモン ● Problems in the Town

How much exposure is indecent?

Summer is a time when everybody feels a certain sense of freedom. And young girls tend to express this in the way they dress.

That's natural perhaps, but is there not a little too much "freedom" in girls' summer attire recently? Showing a little bra, or showing a little panty, these "**show-off undergarments**" seem to be all the rage. Some girls even seem comfortable with their breasts or buttocks half-exposed. It rather makes it difficult for a man to know where he's supposed to look...

Of course, if you just walk down the street stark naked it's a serious **crime of public indecency**; but are these **self-exposing girls** in any danger of getting arrested? We asked the press office of the National Police Agency.

"Of course you'll get arrested if you go running down the street naked, but otherwise, it's just a question of fashion. We've never heard of young girls getting arrested, and there are no clear-cut definitions of what is illegal to show. There is a lot of grey area when it comes to applying the law on public indecency."

This may seem too free a hand in dealing with public lewdness, but this leads us to ask, "What IS indecency anyhow?"

警察庁によると"わいせつ"の明確な**定義**はないらしい。摘発された公然わいせつ罪の内容を見ると、ストリーキング、街中でのAV撮影、ストリップ小屋でのショーなどだから、たしかにこの中に露出ギャルを入れるのは無理がある。
　では「**軽犯罪法違反**」ではどうだろう。ノゾキや立ちションなども該当するものだが、その第1条にこんな項目がある。
　「公衆の目に触れるような場所で公衆に嫌悪の情を催させるような仕方でしり、ももその他身体の一部をみだりに露出した者」
　これならどうだ。
　「難しいでしょうね。たとえ乳首や乳房が見えていても、ファッションだと言われればそれまでです」（同広報室）
　つまりどんなに露出が過激でも、それがファッションであれば問題なしというわけだ。
　しかし"露出ファッション"と"露出趣味"の違いはどこにあるのか。
　その点について、ある女性誌ライターは「**オシャレならファッション、ダサければ露出趣味**」と言う。
　これまたあいまいな境界線だが、ならば男もオシャレだと主張すればパンツ一枚で街を歩いてもイイってこと？　露出ギャルがウヨウヨいる街をパトロール中のおまわりさんに聞いてみたら……。
　「**ダメですよ**。それがファッションだと思いますか？　常識的に考えてください」
　男は注意されるのに、女はおとがめなし。なんだか割り切れない思いが残る。

街中のギモン ● **Problems in the Town**

According to the NPA, there is NO clear **definition** of indecency. Examples of cases which have been prosecuted for indecency include streaking, public display of pornographic materials, unlicensed strip shows, etc. It seems that self-exposing fashion is off the hook.

How about the **Minor Offense Law**, which covers crimes such as peeping and urinating in public? Article 1 defines "petty offenses" as: "Behavior or exposure of the body which invokes public disgust in a place open to public view." So have we got them now? Let's ask the NPA again.

"That's a tough one . . . Even if a womans' breasts or nipples are exposed, if she can insist it's just fashion, then that's the end of it."

So it seems that anything goes as long as it's "fashion." But is there a difference between "exposure as fashion" and "exposure as indecency?" We asked a writer for a women's magazine.

"If it's **tasteful**, it's fashion: if it's not, then it's indecent."

This isn't a very easy-to-grasp definition either. So if a man walks around town in nothing but a pair of briefs, is he OK as long as he insists it's fashion? We asked a police officer on patrol in a part of town where the girls are not exactly known for their public modesty.

"**No way**! Do you think you could really call that fashion? Please be reasonable!" he scolded us.

So men get scolded and women are free to do as they please. Something just doesn't seem to be right, but what can you do?

「猛犬注意」の札の効果は!?

　「セールスお断り」とか「猛犬注意」といった札を玄関や門に張りつけている家をよく見かける。アレは**効果がある**ものなんだろうか？

　顔見知りの**訪問販売**のセールスマンに聞いた。

　「ああ、あれですか。普通の人にはわかンないでしょうね」とまずはナゾめいた笑みをもらす。

　ん？　と思っていると、こう続けた。

　「われわれの仲間では、ああいう札が張ってある家は絶好の狙い目なのです」

　「猛犬注意」の札のある家の多くは犬など飼っていなかったり、いてもかわいらしい室内犬だったりするのだという。

　「セールスお断り」の家もチャイムを押すと、「札が見えないの!?」などとインターホン越しに怒鳴られる例はまずない。丁寧に応対してくれて、中にはお茶まで出したうえに商品を買ってくれることも少なくないのだそうだ。なぜなのか？

　「何も札を張ってない家が**10軒に1軒の確率**で物を買ってくれるとすると、張ってある家は5軒は買ってくれます」と訪問販売のセールスマンは言う。これではなんのお守りにもならない。何が狙いで張っているのだろうか。セールスマンは言った。

街中のギモン ● Problems in the Town

Do "Beware of Dog" signs really do any good?

You often see homes with signs reading "Salesmen Need Not Call" or "Beware of Dog" posted at the front entrance. Do these signs actually **serve some purpose**? We tried asking an acquaintance of ours who works in **door-to-door sales**.

"Ah, those . . . ," he said with a smile. "Most people probably don't know what those are all about, I suppose." Finally he let us in on the truth: "In this line of business, people with things like that posted on their door are your best customers."

Most people advising you to "beware of dog" actually have no dog . . . or a small poodle at best.

You also might expect people with "Salesmen Need Not Call" posted on their doors to greet salesmen with; "What! Can't you read the sign!?" But such is not the case. They are, in fact, polite and hospitable. Some even make tea for their "guest" and actually buy some of the products being offered. But why?

"With houses with no kind of sign like that on the door, you've got a **one-in-ten chance** of getting them to buy something. But when you see 'Salesmen Need Not Call,' you know your chances are about 50/50," our salesman friend tells us. If these are the people who are actually buying this stuff, what's

「人がよさそうなタイプが多いんですよ。何度も不必要なモノを買わされて、息子さんや娘さんが頭にきて張ったんだと思います」

目に見えるような2世帯住宅の光景だ。「おばあちゃん、またこんなモノ買って」と息子や娘にこぼされているのだろう。

つまり、ベテランのセールスマンから見ると「猛犬注意」や「セールスお断り」の札が張ってある家庭は、「この家はセールスを撃退できない人が留守番しています」と告知しているようなものなのだ。

セールスマンは言う。

「会社の玄関に張ってあるとわれわれも入りにくいのですが、一般の家庭は張らない**ほうがいい**と思いますよ」と。

マンションの入り口で見かけることもあるが、こちらのほうは、「いちいち気にしていたら**商売になりません**」だって。

せっかくの札はなんの役にも立たないということか。

こんな札も全く役立たず
Warning or invitation?

the point in them telling salesmen "not to call"?

"They're all really nice people. The only thing I can think is that their son or daughter must have gotten fed up with them buying so many unnecessary things, and put the sign up as a measure of defense." Could this be another result of adult children living with their parents? "Mom, I can't believe you bought all this junk again!"

In any case, in the eyes of the veteran salesman, "Salesmen Need Not Call," means "Aha! Here's a person who can't say no!"

According to our friend: "If you see a sign like that at the entrance of a business, it's a good idea not to go in, but for residences, I think these people would **be better off with** no sign on their door at all!"

"What do you do if you see signs like these on the entrance of an apartment building?" we asked.

"Ignore them. If we worried that much about things, we'd **never make a living**."

In conclusion, we must sadly report that these signs are rather less effective than you might have thought.

街頭の占い師。
資格はいるのか？ 収入は？

繁華街を通ると「手相」「人相」などの看板を掲げた**占い師**をよく見かける。アレをやるには何か**資格**がいるのだろうか？ また、どれくらいの収入になるのか？ まず、街頭に店を出す「占い師」を直撃した。

「ここで商売をするには何か資格がいるのですか？」と単刀直入に聞くと、30代半ばの男は、「そういうことは私に聞かれてもわかりません。責任者に聞いてもらわないと」と言うだけ。責任者がどこにいるのかも教えてくれない。

仕方なく知人に「占い師」を紹介してもらった。この道二十余年という彼は現在、喫茶店の一角を借りて**商売をしている**という。記者の質問に彼は簡単に答えてくれた。

「繁華街の街頭で商売しているのは、占いの会社みたいなところに所属または登録した人です」

あらかじめ**地元のテキ屋**に話をつけてあるので、いつも同じ場所で商売できるというのだ。

「じゃ、リストラされたサラリーマンが占いを勉強して商売にしようというのは難しい？」

記者は聞いた。

「街頭でやるのは難しいけど、最近は志願者が多い

街中のギモン ● Problems in the Town

Do sidewalk palm-readers have some kind of qualification? How much do they make?

Along busy shopping arcades you often see **fortune-tellers** with signs out reading "Palm Reading" or "Fortunes told." Do you need some kind of **qualification** to do that work? And to these people actually make any money? First, we tried asking the fortune-teller at work on the street.

We asked him straight. "Do you need some kind of qualification to do this kind of work?" The man, in his mid 30s, replied: "I'm afraid I can't tell you that. You'll have to speak with the person in charge." But when we asked who was in charge, he wouldn't tell us.

We were, however, able to gain audience to a more cooperative fortune-teller through the introduction of a friend. This man has been in this line of work for over 20 years, and currently rents a corner of a tea room in which to **set up shop**.

"The people telling fortunes on the street are usually registered with some kind of fortune-telling agency, which arranges with the **local peddlers** for someone to be able to conduct business there regularly."

"Well then, if a laid-off company worker wants to go into fortune-telling, is there any chance for him to make a living?" we asked.

"It's hard to find a job telling fortunes on the street, but

んですよ」

と占い師。彼の元にも占いの基本を習いたいという人が少なからずやってくるので教えることもあるのだという。

「本気でやれば、半年くらいで**基本は**覚えられます。でも、ビジネスとしてやって食えるようになるのは100人に1人か2人ですね」

ある程度占いができるようになれば、どこかの組織に出店場所を紹介してもらう方法もあるし、自分で喫茶店などと**交渉して**「占いコーナー」を設置させる手も。

「私は何軒かの喫茶店でやらせてもらっていますが、年間ざっと5000人見ています」と占い師は言った。

1人3000円の見料として年に1500万円の売り上げ。

「けっこういい商売ですね」と言うと、「いやいや、政治家や財界人と契約して、アドバイザーになるくらいでないと一流とはいえません」との答え。大儲けは難しくても、身過ぎ世過ぎのためには「占い師」もよさそうな気がしてきた。

街中のギモン ● Problems in the Town

recently there have been more and more requests from people interested in learning about this work." This man also has a good number of "students" who are trying to learn the basics of fortune-telling, so teaching is also a source of income.

"A serious student can **pick up the basics** in six months or so. But there are only one or two people out of a hundred who are actually able to make a living out of it," he says.

After you've learned the basics, you can apply with a fortune-telling agency to try to get your own spot somewhere on the street, or you can also try to **negotiate with** a tea room to set up a "fortune-telling corner" in their shop.

"I currently work in a number of tea rooms, and I see 5,000 clients a year," this man says. And he gets ¥3,000 per client. That's ¥15,000,000 a year.

When we complimented him on his income, "No, it's not that great, really. Unless you can get on as an 'advisor' with some politician or **business tycoon**, you can't really consider yourself as having 'made it' as a fortune-teller," he confessed. So it may be hard to really make a fortune, but if you're lucky, telling fortunes may be a better job than you expected!

おみくじはなぜどこの神社でも同じなのか?

おみくじは、どこの寺社でも似たようなものが使われているのはどうしてだろう?

大きな寺社では自前のおみくじを用意しているところも多い。例えば明治神宮のおみくじは「**大吉**」や「**吉**」などの**記載**がなく、明治天皇の和歌が記されているだけのもの。

京都の貴船神社のおみくじは何も書かれておらず、境内の泉に**浮かべる**と文字が浮かんで見える仕掛けになっている。これは貴船神社が水の神様を祀っているため。なかなか情緒がある。

しかし小さな神社などでは、ほとんどが既製品を使っている。最大手は山口県周南市にある二所山田神社の関連会社である「女子道社」だ。

「20種類のおみくじを卸しているのですが、具体的なシェアについてはわかりません」(二所山田神社)とのことだが、寺社関係者によると、全国の6割以上のおみくじが女子道社製だという。二所山田神社がおみくじ作りを始めたのは明治39(1906)年。**初代宮司**の宮本重胤氏が、社会における女性の役割の大きさを訴えた機関誌「女子道」を発刊したことがきっ

Why are *omikuji* fortunes the same at all the Shinto shrines?

Have you noticed that the *omikuji* fortunes you get at Buddhist temples and Shinto shrines are more or less the same wherever you go?

Most if the big temples and shrines have their own *omikuji* slips. For example, at Meiji Shrine, your fortune won't bear the usual **proclamations** of "**Great Blessing**" or "**Blessing**," just wakapoems composed by the Emperor Meiji. At Kibune Shrine in Kyoto, you won't "see" anything printed on your fortune at first. The slips are printed with a special ink that only becomes visible when you **set it afloat** in the shrine's fountain. This is because Kibune Shrine **honors** a god of water—rather an impressive trick.

Most smaller shrines, however, use commercially printed fortunes. The biggest printer of these fortunes is Joshidosha, an affiliated company of Nisho Yamada Shrine in Shunan, Yamaguchi Prefecture. Nisho Yamada Shrine says: "We have 20 different types of *omikuji* fortunes in distribution, but we don't really keep track of what our exact share of the market is." But persons connected with the affairs of temples and shrines estimate that over 60% of all *omikuji* fortunes used in Japan are made by Joshidosha. Nisho Yamada Shrine's fortune printing business began with its **founding priest**, Shigetane

かけだったという。機関誌発行の**資金調達**にと、その印刷工場を利用したおみくじ作りが始まった。

おみくじは1番から50番、または1番から100番までが1セットになったものが主流だが、その中の文言の1つでも時代に合わなくなったら、1セット全部を書き改めているそうだ。宮司が**お清め**をして社にこもり、神の啓示を受けながら執筆するそうで、1セット書き上げるのに1カ月かかる。その後、工場で印刷し、お清めをして神社に祭られてから全国に運ばれる。

中には英文のおみくじもあるそうで、海外にも出荷されているそうだ。ちなみに、おみくじにはたいがい和歌が書かれているが、これも歌人であった初代宮司の発案だそうだ。

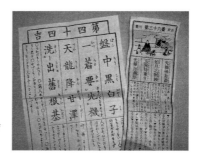

おみくじは占いではなく、神仏の励ましの言葉だとか

Omikuji fortunes represent words of encouragement from the gods, not mere divination.

Miyamoto. He started the business as a way to **raise funds** for his shrine's magazine, "Joshido" (The Woman's Path), dedicated to increasing awareness of the importance of women's role in society.

The *omikuji* fortunes usually come in sets from 1 to 50 or from 1 to 100, but if even one phrase used in a set of fortunes is found to be unsuitable to the times we live in, they rewrite the entire set. The priest **performs an ablution ritual**, and then retreats into the shrine to receive the word of the gods to record for the fortunes. The process of rewriting an entire set of fortunes can take up to a full month. The fortunes are then printed and undergo a purification ritual at the shrine before being shipped all over the country.

You might be surprised to find out that their customers are not limited only to Japan, and amongst their wide variety of fortunes, you'll even find English-language sets. Also, almost all the fortune slips are inscribed with *waka* poetry, which is also said to be the idea of Priest Miyamoto.

道路のトンネル照明に オレンジと白があるのはなぜ？

　トンネルの照明といえばオレンジ色が**定番**だ。しかし、最近は白い照明もよく見かける。なぜトンネル照明の色は2種類あるのか？

　「オレンジ色の照明は**低圧ナトリウム灯**と呼ばれるもので、**排ガス**の中でも光が遠くまで届きやすい。そのうえ低コストなのです」と言うのは国土交通省だ。

　白い光は排ガスに乱反射しやすく、トンネル内では視界が曇ってしまうのだとか。

　「しかし、低圧ナトリウム灯には、路面の白いセンターラインが追い越し禁止を意味するオレンジ色に見えてしまう欠点があります。数年前に明るくて安価な**蛍光灯**が開発されたので、交通量が少なかったり**換気設備**が整ったトンネルに限って蛍光灯に交換しています。白い照明は、トンネル内が自然な色に見える新型の蛍光灯なんです」（国土交通省）

　白い光でも**光量**が強ければ乱反射しにくいそうだが、排ガスが多すぎるトンネルでは、いまでも蛍光灯は使えない。状況に応じて使い分けている、というわけだ。

　「従来は、高速道路のトンネル照明はすべてオレン

Why do highway tunnels have both orange and white lighting?

When it comes to lighting in highway tunnels, orange is the **norm**. But nowadays, you also see tunnels with white lighting once in a while. Why do they use two types of lighting?

According to the Ministry of Land, Infrastructure and Transport, "The orange lights you see are **low-pressure sodium lamps**. The light from these lamps cuts well through the **exhaust gas** in the tunnels, and the operational costs are comparatively low." White light, in contrast, is easily refracted by the exhaust gas, resulting in lowered visibility in the tunnels. "But the drawback to low-pressure sodium is that it can make a regular white dividing line look orange, which would indicate a no-passing zone. A few years back, however, low-cost and higher-brightness **fluorescent lamps** were developed, so in tunnels where the traffic isn't too heavy and tunnels with **ventilation systems** for the exhaust gas, we've been switching over to white. These new fluorescent lamps allow more natural visibility in the tunnels."

With sufficient **luminosity**, the white light is resistant to refraction, but these new fluorescent lamps still can't be used in tunnels where the exhaust gas is too heavy, so the choice of which color to use depends on the circumstances.

According to East Nippon Expressway: "Traditionally,

ジの低圧ナトリウム灯でしたが、1998年から2005年4月までに、全国の15％のトンネルで蛍光灯にしました。高速道路のトンネルは排気設備が整っているので、蛍光灯のほうが**利点**は多いのです」（東日本高速道路㈱）

　ちなみに、蛍光灯は大きさによって1個1万～2万円で、**設置用ボックス**が1個10万～40万円。100灯を交換すれば軽く1000万円を超えてしまう高価なシロモノだ。

街中のギモン ● **Problems in the Town**

all expressways used orange low-pressure sodium lamps, but from 1998 to April 2005, 15% of tunnels nationwide were switched over to white. The tunnels on the expressways are equipped with ventilation systems, so the **advantages** of fluorescent lamps win out."

And if you're wondering how much these things cost, the fluorescent lamps run from ¥10,000 to ¥20,000 apiece, depending on the size; and the **fixtures** they're installed in, from ¥100,000 to ¥400,000. So to replace 100 lamps runs easily ¥10 million! It kind of makes it hard to complain about those toll fees.

セーラー服が減っている理由は？

学校帰りの女子中高生。学生服のデザインもさまざまで、街はさながら制服の見本市だが、近頃はあまり**セーラー服**を見かけない。なぜか？

「1980年代半ばに全国的な"制服のモデルチェンジブーム"が起こって以来、セーラー服を採用している学校は年々減っています」と言うのは、『女子高制服図鑑・首都圏版』（弓立社）の著書がある、イラストレーターで制服研究家の森伸之氏だ。

森氏のいう"モデルチェンジブーム"は、都内のある古い私立女子高が突然セーラー服をブレザーとタータンチェックのスカートに替えたのがきっかけ。以前からセーラー服には、"**重ね着**ができない""脱ぎにくい"など**機能**面への不満の声があり、そこに"新しい制服で他校と**差別化**したい"という学校側の思惑が加わって"脱セーラー服"の波は全国に広がった。その結果、今はブレザーが主流になっている。

そもそもセーラー服はイギリス海軍の水兵服が発

街中のギモン ● Problems in the Town

Why are sailor suit uniforms on the decline?

In town, you can see a wide variety of girls school uniforms as junior high and high school students make their way home. But why is it that you don't see very much of the **sailor suit uniforms** that you used to?

According to Nobuyuki Mori, uniform researcher, illustrator, and author of the Graphic Encyclopedia of Girls' High School Uniforms/Tokyo Edition (Yudachi Press), "Since the mid 1980s when there was a rush of shool uniform changes, the number of schools using sailor suit uniforms has been decreasing every year."

What Mr. Mori means by "a rush of school uniform changes" began when one of Tokyo's old private schools abandoned sailor suits for blazers and tartan check skirts. There had always been complaints about the **functionality** of sailor suit uniforms: not being suitable for **wearing layers**, being difficult to get undressed, etc. So when one school tried to take advantage of this by changing the school uniforms to **distinguish** itself from its competition, it triggered an "anti-sailor suit" wave of uniform changes across the country. The result is the large number of high schools in blazers you see nowadays.

These uniforms were first designed by the British navy,

祥。日本では明治時代に日本海軍が同じ**水兵服**として**取り入れた**のが最初だ。学校では大正時代に福岡女学院が体操服として取り入れたのが初めてとされる。以降、物資不足の戦中・戦後の一時期を除けば、女子学生の制服はほとんどがセーラー服だった。

 それが今では、「3割程度」(森氏＝前出) という落ち込みよう。しかもこれは比較的"セーラー服率"が高いとされる、都内の制服のある私立中学・高校での話で、全国だと「2割程度」(学生服生地メーカー)にまで下がる。大手学生服メーカーの尾崎商事 (カンコー学生服を展開) も、

「新しく作る場合は圧倒的にブレザーが多い。伝統的なセーラー服を採用する学校は、まずありませんね」(広報担当者)

 セーラー服は**絶滅**してしまうのか？

「東京女学館や白百合、学習院女子といったセーラー服が伝統の**名門校**は、今後もモデルチェンジしないでしょう」(森氏＝前出)

 それに女子高生たちの間でも、実はセーラー服への回帰現象が起こりつつあるという。

「女子高生へのアンケートでは、実はセーラー服が一番人気。近頃は襟をセーラー型にした"セーラー服風"ブレザーにも人気が集まっています」(尾崎商事広報担当者)

 セーラー服好きなアナタ。まずは一安心ですゾ！

and they were first **adopted** in Japan as **naval uniforms** during the Meiji period. The first recorded use in Japanese schools is in the Taisho period as the physical education uniform for the Fukuoka Girls' Academy. Since then, with the exception of periods of material rationing during and after WWII, sailor suits had been the standard girls school uniforms.

Mr. Mori estimates that currently only around 30% of private junior high and high schools using uniforms in the Tokyo area use sailor suits. And when we asked a school uniform textile maker for a nationwide figure, their estimate was 20%. According to industry leader Ozaki Shoji (creators of the "Kanko" brand school uniform), "When schools go to make new uniforms nowadays, they almost always go with blazers. No one wants the traditional sailor suits now."

So is the sailor suit going to **become extinct**?

"**Prestigious schools** with a tradition of sailor suit uniforms like Tokyo Jogakkan Middle and High School, Shirayuri, and Gakushuin Girls' Senior and Junior High School are less likely to change their uniforms," Mr. Mori says.

And it seems as though the sailor suit is making a comeback among high school girls as well. "A survey of high school girls shows that the sailor suit is actually most popular. Recently, 'sailor-style' blazers, with collar designs similar to sailor suits, have also been gaining in popularity," Ozaki Shoji's public relations department reports.

So for the men out there who miss seeing girls in sailor suits like in the old days, there's still hope!

郊外の駅前のたこ焼き屋はだれでもできるのか？

記者の住む私鉄の沿線には夜になると**軽トラック**やワゴン車でやってきて店を出す「たこ焼き屋」が多い。

駅の**ロータリー**の中や、目の前の道路で商売しているが、だれでもできるものなのだろうか？

郊外の某駅で「たこ焼き」の店を出しているオジサンに聞いた。

「だれでもできるわけじゃないよ。オレたちは"寅さん"と同じ**テキ屋**だからね。やはりこのへんを仕切っている元締にそれなりの**あいさつ**をしないと」

いったい、どんなあいさつをするのだろうか。

「オレはもうこの道で古株だから、仲間内の冠婚葬祭の"**義理**"を欠かさないことくらい。素人がやるのだったら**アルバイト**から始めるしかないな」

とつれない返事。

この店で働く"若い衆"の日当は1万円くらいだそうだ。

「もうかるんですか?」と聞いた。
「**商売になる**のは"お祭り"や運動会だね」

街中のギモン ● Problems in the Town

Can anyone set up a *takoyaki* stand out in front of a train station?

Around train stations in the suburbs, you see people selling *takoyaki* from the backs of station wagons and **small pickup** trucks. In the middle of a **roundabout** or just parked on the side of the road, they're open for business. Can anybody just open up shop like this?

We found one old man selling *takoyaki* out in front of a suburban station and asked him.

"No, it's not something anyone can just up and do. We're **peddlers**, just like 'Tora-san' in the movies. You've got to **be on friendly terms with** the people running things in the area to be able to work like this."

So how are we supposed to get friendly with these bigshots? Do we just walk up and bid them good-day?

"I've been doing this a long time, and there are a lot of '**obligations**' (*giri* in Japanese) to the people around me. Knowing how to give gifts properly when people have weddings or funerals is just part of staying in business. If someone with no connections wants to get into this work, the only way is to start out as **part-time help**," he continued, adding that his part-time "youngsters" make around ¥10,000 a day.

"You make much?" we asked.

"It's the festivals and school sports festivals that **keep**

お祭りがあると普段の場所での商売は休んで店を出すというが、この時は2日間で3万円くらいの"**ショバ代**"を**元締**に払う。ほかに「バッテリー」を借りると3000円必要だが、これも「自分の物を持っていますから」と断るわけにはいかないのだという。

　要は2日間で3万3000円は**必要経費**がかかるのだ。それでも1日10万円、20万円と売れることは**珍しくない**ので"若い衆"に日当を払っても利益は出る。

　もっと"オイシイ"のは小学校の運動会。校門の外に「たこ焼き」「焼きそば」「**あんずあめ**」などの店を出すのには学校にあいさつするだけで済む。
「まぁ先生には商売する品物をプレゼントするだけだね」
とオジサンは言った。
「お金はかからないんですか?」と記者が聞くと、少し困った様子だったが、こう話してくれた。
「多少は使うよ。でも渡し方が難しいんだよ。**露骨に金を出す**と後で問題になることもあるから」

　オジサンが**声をひそめて**明かしてくれたのは、PTAに「掃除代」の名目で渡す、という手口。祝儀袋の上書きは「**寸志**」なのだという。

街中のギモン ● Problems in the Town

us in business." When there's a festival, they don't open up shop at their usual location for 2 days, but they have to pay a "**protection fee**" of ¥30,000 to "**the people running things**." They also get charged ¥3,000 to borrow a battery for the event, and it's considered unwise to refuse it because you've already got your own.

So they're looking at ¥33,000 in **overhead**, but sales of ¥100,000 and even ¥200,000 in a single day are **commonplace**, so they make a handsome profit even after paying off their "youngsters."

The elementary school sports festivals are even a better **killing**. The only overhead officially needed to set up shop selling *takoyaki*, *yakisoba* or **candied apples** is a word of greeting to the school. "Well, actually I do usually give the teachers some *takoyaki* as a gift," the old man said.

"You really don't give them any money?" we asked.

At this question, he looked as though he didn't know what to say, but he finally explained. "Yeah, I give them a little bit, but giving can be complicated. If you just hand money to people out **in the open**, it can turn into a problem later."

He later **mutedly** explained that he gives it to the PTA as a gift for "clean-up expenses." The money envelope he hands to them bears the inscription "**A Token of Appreciation**."

水族館の海水は どこから運んでいる？

最近は第3次水族館ブームといわれているが、水族館の海水はどこから持ってきているのか？

実は日本は世界一の水族館大国。『決定版!! 全国水族館ガイド』の著者で新江ノ島水族館顧問の中村元氏は言う。

「水族館は世界に約500カ所ありますが、そのうち約100カ所が日本にあり、年間3000万人が水族館を訪れます。入館者数も断トツで世界一です」

水族館にとって重要な問題が海水の**管理**と**補充**。魚の種類によって水温や**水質**を細かく管理する必要があるのだ。では、その海水をどこから持ってきているのか。水族館の立地条件などによって違うが、一般的なのは近くの海から引いてくる方法。

「**海岸線**にあるので、海に向かって取水路が引かれています。潮の満ち引きを利用して、1日約1000トンの海水を取り入れています」（新江ノ島水族館広報室）

一方、**内陸**や、東京湾のように海水を取るには適さない場所にある水族館では、トレーラーで海水を運んでいるケースが多い。葛西臨海水族園では、海運会社と契約。八丈島で荷物を降ろした**貨物船**が、

街中のギモン ● Problems in the Town

Where does aquarium water come from?

Recently, public aquariums are all the rage in Japan. Where does the water for these facilities come from?

You may be surprised to find out that Japan is a world leader when it comes to public aquariums. New Enoshima Aquarium advisor Hajime Nakamura, author of *This Is the Last Word!! A Guide to the Aquariums of Japan*, says, "There are 500 public aquariums in the world. About 100 of these are in Japan, with 30 million people visiting them a year. The number of visitors is by far the highest in the world."

For aquariums, one of the most important issues is **maintaining** and **supplying** water. Water temperature and **composition** must also be controlled precisely for each kind of fish. Where do they bring the water from? It depends on each aquarium's location, but generally, they draw water from the nearest seashore.

"Our facility is on the **seashore**. We've laid pipelines to the sea, and by utilizing the power of the tide, we take in about 1,000 tons of water a day," says New Enoshima Aquarium PR.

On the other hand, at aquariums where the location is inappropriate for getting water this way for instance, **inland** locations and Tokyo Bay—they transport water by trailer. Kasai Rinkai Aquarium has a contract with a marine

船を安定させるため帰路に積む「バラスト水」を利用している。船が東京湾に着くと、海水をトレーラーに乗せ換えて運ぶ。1カ月に運ばれてくる海水の量は約3000トン。輸送費など含め、年間1億5000万円がかかるとか。

　また、「**人工海水**」を利用する水族館もある。栃木県なかがわ水遊園では、海水と同じ成分を調合して作る「海水パウダー」を地元の**井戸水**に溶かして使っている。
　「人工海水はコストが低く、水に病原菌が混じる危険性が小さいというメリットがあるんです」（同広報）

　週末はどの水族館もにぎわっている。
　「都会生活の"渇き"を癒すために水族館が必要とされているのかもしれません」（中村氏＝前出）
　たまには水槽を満たす海水に注目して水族館巡りをしてみては？

transportation company to bring "ballast water" from cargo ships which unload their freight at Hachijojima Island. When the **cargo ships** arrive back at port in Tokyo Bay, the water is pumped into tank trailers and driven out. They transport about 3,000 tons of water a month, at a cost of around ¥150 million a year.

In the meantime, some aquariums use "**synthetic seawater.**" Tochigi Nakagawa Aquarium dissolves "sea-water powder," which has the same composition as real seawater, into **well water**.

"The advantage of synthetic seawater is that it's inexpensive and safe because it is resistant to infection by bacteria," says their PR department.

Every weekend, all aquariums are busy. "I guess people need aquariums to relieve their minds from the stresses of urban life," says Mr. Nakamura.

Next time you visit an aquarium, see if you can't catch a glimpse of the trucks bringing in the water?

エスカレーターで右側を空けて乗るのはなぜ？

東京の駅のエスカレーターなどで見かける"右側を通行者のために空ける"行為。どうしてこうなったのか？

確かにこの"風習"、うっかり右側に立とうものなら後ろからにらまれるほど徹底している。

実際そんなルールはあるのだろうか。

「そういうお願いをしたことは一切ありません」とは東京メトロの広報担当者。いつから始まったのかについても不明だという。他の鉄道会社にも聞いたが答えは同じだった。

要は利用者が**自発的**に行っている"暗黙のルール"のよう。だが、なぜ右側なのか？

「基本的に駅舎内は**左側通行**。だから追い越す人は右側を通るのではないですか」（東京メトロ）

一方、東京とは逆に関西では"左側"を空けるのが常識とされている。

これについては諸説あるが、「関西ではエスカレーターの降り口の左側に改札やホームがあることが多いから歩きやすい」や「関西人には**左利き**が少ない。

街中のギモン ● **Problems in the Town**

Why do people keep the right side of the escalator open?

Try taking the escalator at Tokyo Station, and there's one thing you'll definitely notice: everyone stands on the left side. This "habit" is followed so completely that you'll be bothered by people trying to walk by if you stop on the right-hand side.

Is this some kind of rule?

"It's no rule and we've never requested passengers to comply with it," says Tokyo Metro PR. No one knows when it started, and the other railway companies all give the same answer.

So it seems to be a kind of **unspoken rule** which passengers follow **voluntarily**. But why stand on the left rather than on the right?

"In the station building, people are usually supposed to **keep to the left** in the passageways. So, people who walk faster walk on the right side," the Tokyo Metro offers as one possible reason.

On the other hand, unlike Tokyo, in Kansai it is common to keep the left-hand side open.

There are various theories about this. One states that "in Kansai, ticket gates and platforms are often located on the left side of the escalators. That's why it is easier for people to keep

だからみんな右手で手すりにつかまるから」など、どれも**あやふや**。はっきりした理由はわからない。

ところで、このエスカレーターの追い抜き、以前から「急いでいる人のために空けるべき」という声もあれば、「危険だからやめるべきだ」という声もあり、ちょっとした**論争**になっている。

エスカレーターを歩くことは実際に危険なのか？
「本当です。エスカレーターは突然急ブレーキがかかることもあり、その場合は大事故につながる可能性があります」（日本エレベータ協会）
追い越していいのかダメなのか、暗黙ではなくハッキリとしたルールを早く作ったほうがよいのでは？

関東は右、関西は左を空けることが多いらしい……

Further evidence of the Tokyo/Kansai rivalry.
Which side of the escalator do you stand on?

to the right." Another questionable theory states that "there are fewer **left-handed people** in Kansai, so people keep to the right so that they can grab the handrail more easily." And so on. But each theory is **inconclusive**, and the real reason remains a mystery.

By the way, passing on escalators has become a point of **controversy** recently. Some say, "We should keep one side of the escalator open for those who are in a hurry," while others insist that "walking on escalators is dangerous, so there's no point in going out of one's way to accommodate them."

Is it really dangerous to walk on an escalator? "Yes, if an escalator suddenly stops, it can lead to serious accidents." (Japan Escalator Association)

Don't you think rather than an unspoken rule, we'd better actually decide whether it's safe to pass people as we hurry our way up the escalator?

Part 3

鉄ちゃんのギモン
Problems with Trains

電車のシート、1人当たりの幅の基準は？

電車の座席。「7人がけ」とか「3人がけ」というけれど、1人当たりの幅はどのように設定されているのか。定員どおりに座るとどうも狭苦しいのだが……。

現在、JRや主な私鉄の通勤電車の座席1人当たりの幅は約45センチ。電車の座席の幅にはJIS規格があり、1人当たりの幅が43センチと決められているのだ。

これは昭和54（1979）年に制定されたもので**座席定員**を算出するための標準になる数値だ。JISC（日本工業標準調査会）によれば、「43センチは**人間工学**に基づいて独自に設定されたもの。ただしあくまでも**最低基準**です」とのこと。以前はほとんどの鉄道会社がこの定員を算出するための標準である43センチに設定していた。座席の幅を決めているのは、あくまでも鉄道事業者や、鉄道車両メーカー。車両の刷新とともに各社とも座席の幅を広げる努力をしてはいるようだが、実感としては45センチでも**狭い**。

JIS規格で43センチと決められる以前はどうだったかというと、昭和33（1958）年に旧国鉄から発刊された『鉄道技術発達史』によれば、明治から昭和初

鉄ちゃんのギモン ● Problems with Trains

What's the standard for deciding how many people should fit into that train seat?

Above bench seats on trains you often see, "7 **Passenger Capacity**" or "3 Passenger Capacity," but just how much space are they allowing per person in their calculations here? It always seems a bit cramped when that 7th or 3rd person squeezes their way in.

Currently, the standard for JR and the major private rail lines is around 45 cm per person. The Japan Industrial Standards (JIS) define the space for one person on train seats as 43 cm.

This figure was set in 1979 and became the standard for calculating train **seating capacity**. According to the Japan Industrial Standards Committee (JISC), "The 43 cm figure was derived from **ergonomics findings**, but in reality it only serves as a **minimum estimate**." Since then, almost all rail companies used this figure to calculate seating capacity. But the final decision as to seating widths lies with the rail companies or car manufacturers themselves. Since then it seems that they have been trying to increase seating widths little by little—but even 45 cm still feels a little **tight**.

What was the situation before the JIS 43 cm standard? According to the *History of Rail Technology Development* published by the former Japanese National Railways in 1958, from

期にかけての**通勤電車**の座席1人当たりの幅は「2等車で53センチないし60センチ、3等車で42.5センチないし46.5センチ」が標準。当時の3等車が現在の通勤電車に**該当する**そうだから、1人当たりの幅は昔も今も同程度だ。体こそ今より小さかっただろうが、空調設備がなかった分、衣服はかさばっていたとの見方もあり、"窮屈さ"は今と変わらなかったようだ。

「むやみに幅を広げればいいというものではありません。今以上に広げても、結局空いた隙間(すきま)に人が割り込んでよけいに窮屈になる可能性がありますから」(JISC担当者)

1人ひとりが微妙な隙間を空けて座ると、どうしても定員どおりにはいかない。つまり現在の45センチは、より多くの人が座るための"**適正幅**"であって、少々狭くても我慢するほかないようだ。

適正幅に区切られたシート
Seats divided by the ideal width.

鉄ちゃんのギモン ● **Problems with Trains**

the Meiji through Showa periods the standard per person for commuter trains was "53 to 60 cm in 2nd class and 42.5 to 46.5 cm in 3rd class cars." So it seems today's **commuter trains** would **correspond to** the 3rd class trains of the past, and the seating widths haven't changed much over the years. People back then were smaller than today's Japanese, but it has been observed that without heating in the cars like today, the passengers of the past used to bundle up rather thickly in winter, and the sense of tightness was probably little different than today.

"It isn't just a question of 'the wider, the better.' Even if the seating width were to be widened now, there is always the chance that people would try to work their way into the resulting gaps, making it even tighter than it is now," says the JISC.

When people leave even a small gap between themselves and their neighbors, it keeps the trains from seating full capacity, and while the 45 cm standard may feel a bit close, it seems to be the **ideal width** for the greatest number of people to sit comfortably . . . So grin and bear it!

駅構内のチャイム音は
何を知らせているのか？

鉄道駅構内で、「ピーン、ポーン」というチャイム音を聞くことがある。いったい、何の音なのか？

この「ピーン、ポーン」というチャイム音。鳴っている場所は改札口やホームなどまちまちで、鳴らない駅もある。

全駅でチャイム音を鳴らしている小田急電鉄によると、「チャイム音は、**目が不自由な方向けの誘導音**で、**改札口**の位置を知らせるものです」とのこと。JR東日本も、「鳴らす場所は基本的には改札口で、駅によっては階段でも鳴らしています」と言う。チャイム音は、JRなどを中心に、古くから自主的に設置されていたが、都内のほかの鉄道で本格的に普及し始めたのは、2000年の"**交通バリアフリー法**"制定以降だとか。

「ただ、交通バリアフリー法は新設の駅では**適合**しなくてはいけませんが、既存の駅は努力義務となっていますので十分に普及しているというわけでもないんです。2002年12月のガイドラインでは改札口、エスカレーター、トイレ、ホーム上の階段、地下鉄の地上出入り口に音響・音声案内を行うこととして い

鉄ちゃんのギモン ● Problems with Trains

What are those chime sounds for that you hear in train stations?

As you walk through a train station, you sometimes hear a "ding-dong" like chime sound. They seem almost random. Sometimes you hear them near ticket gates or on the platforms, but some stations have no chime sounds at all. So is there any point to these chimes?

According to Odakyu Electric Railway Co., Ltd., which has chimes in all its stations, "The chime sounds are a **guide to the blind**, indicating the location of **ticket gates**." For East Japan Railway Company, "The chimes are usually located at ticket gates, and some stations also have chimes equipped to indicate the location of staircases. For a number of years, JR and a handful of other rail companies had been installing these chimes independently, but since the introduction of the **Barrier-free Transportation Law** in 2000, other rail companies in the Tokyo area have begun installing chimes in earnest as well.

"However, the Barrier-free Transportation Law only demands full **compliance** for newly built stations," says the Transportation Ecology & Mobility Foundation. "For preexisting stations, rail companies are only required to make an effort to comply with the new standards, so there are still a lot of places where these kinds of guides for the blind are still

ます」(交通エコロジー・モビリティ財団)

　実は、設置基準に定められた誘導音の音色は、チャイムのほかにもうひとつある。ホーム上で階段の位置を知らせる"**鳥の声**"だ。改札口と違う音色をホームで鳴らし、降車直後の移動をスムーズにしようというわけだ。この"鳥の声"、当初は設置駅は少なかったが、JR東日本では2004年度末までに新宿、渋谷、東京など主要駅を中心に48駅に設置した。音によるバリアフリーは少しずつ広がっている。

needed. For example, the guidelines set out in December 2002 state that there should be chimes or voice announcements at ticket gates, escalators, restrooms, platform staircases, and subway entrances."

Actually, the standards indicate another kind of sound that can be used instead of chimes: **bird cries**, to indicate the location of staircases on the platforms. Using a different sound to indicate where people need to go first thing after getting off the train can make it easier for blind people to find their way smoothly through the station and to the ticket gates. At first, there were few stations to adopt the recorded bird cries on the platforms, but by the end of 2004 East Japan Railway had introduced bird cries in some 48 stations, including Shinjuku, Shibuya, and Tokyo. While there still remains much to be done, it's good to see rail companies taking steps to make public transportation more accessible to everyone.

東京駅に向かうのが「上り」列車とは限らない⁉

年末の帰省ラッシュなどで「新幹線上り線乗車率〇〇％」などのニュースを耳にするが、列車の「**上り**」「**下り**」はどうやって決めているのか？

単純に東京駅から地方に向かう列車が「下り」なのかと思ったら、例えばJR中央本線は東京から塩尻までは「下り」だが、塩尻から名古屋までは「上り」に変わる。より大きな都市に向かう列車が「上り」なのか。JR東海に尋ねてみた。

「基本的には東京**方面**に向かう列車が上りです。名古屋と大阪（難波）を結ぶJR関西本線は名古屋方面が上り。どちらが大都市かは微妙ですし……」（JR東海広報室）

東海道本線のように東西に延びる路線はいいが、東海道線に対して、南北方向に交差する**在来線**は、どちらが東京方面か分からないのでは？ JR東日本に聞いてみたところ、

「明確な規定があるかはあいまいで……。鉄道用語

鉄ちゃんのギモン ● Problems with Trains

Not all trains heading for Tokyo are "inbound"?

During the year-end rush when people leave the cities en masse to return to their hometowns, you often hear on the news, "Seats on inbound shinkansen trains are filled to so-and-so percent capacity." What makes one train "**inbound**" and another "**outbound**"?

You may simply think that all trains leaving Tokyo for the provinces are outbound, but consider the fact that, on the JR Chuo Main Line going from Tokyo to Shiojiri is considered outbound, while continuing on from Shiojiri to Nagoya is considered inbound. So should trains heading toward a larger city be considered inbound? Here's the answer JR Central gave us.

"In principle, trains **heading in the direction of** Tokyo are considered inbound. On the JR Kansai Main Line, which connects Nagoya and Osaka (Nanba), trains heading for Nagoya are considered inbound. It's sometimes difficult to judge which should be treated as the 'larger' city . . ."

For lines like the Tokaido Main Line, which stretch out from east to west, this is fine. But for the **conventional lines** which cross the Tokaido line running north and south, isn't it a little difficult to say which direction heads for Tokyo? To this question, a representative from JR East replied, "I don't even

辞典に記載があるかもしれませんが」とのこと。そこで交通博物館に問い合わせてみた。

「線路の起点に向かって運転するのが上り列車、と定められています。起点についての記載は見当たりませんね。戦前の大阪鉄道局編纂の『鉄道用語辞典』によると、帝都（東京）に向かうのが上り、支線においては幹線に向かうのが上り、幹線と幹線を結ぶ支線においては主要な幹線に向かうのが上り列車と定められています」（交通博物館学芸員）

戦前はシンプルに「上り」「下り」を決められたが、鉄道が次々と敷かれていくうちに、同一線内で「上り」「下り」が**混在**したり、東京駅を通過して循環する山手線のように「**内回り**」「**外回り**」と別の呼び方をする路線もできた。東京に向かうか、どちらが主要幹線かはさして重要でなく、現在では「上り」「下り」は運行管理上の問題にすぎないようだ。

赤レンガでおなじみの東京駅丸の内口
Inbound or outbound, you know you're in Tokyo when you see the red brick station.

鉄ちゃんのギモン ● Problems with Trains

know whether any standard exists for that . . . Maybe there's a definition in the *Dictionary of Railway Terminology*."

So we decided to ask the Transportation Museum. "'Inbound' is currently defined as the direction heading toward a rail line's origin, but there's no definition for 'origin.' According to the *Dictionary of Railway Terminology* compiled by the prewar Osaka Railway Bureau, trains heading toward Tokyo are inbound; for **tributary lines**, the direction heading toward the main line is inbound; and for tributaries connecting two main lines, the direction heading toward the more significant of the two main lines is inbound."

Before the war, the definitions were simple, but as the rail system continued to grow, some lines developed with **overlapping** inbound and outbound directions, and others, like the Yamanote Line passing through Tokyo and continuing around in a loop, use terms, like "**inner loop**" and "**outer loop**" to indicate which direction a train is running. Nowadays whether the train is heading for Tokyo, or which is the more major of two main lines, no longer seem to be particularly important questions, and terms like "inbound" and "outbound" seem only to be significant in the realm of operational procedure.

電車に書かれた記号の意味は？

旅先などでは**鉄道マニア**ならずとも気になってしまうのが電車の側面に書かれた「クハ111」などの記号。種別を表すのだろうということは察しがつくが……。

JRによると基本的に「カタカナ記号プラス3ケタの数字」で車両の型式を表しているそうだ。

最初のカタカナは、**運転席**やモーターの有無を表す記号。
「ク」は運転台がある車両（制御車）、「モ」はモーターが付いている車両（中間電動車）、「クモ」は運転台もモーターも付いている車両（制御電動車）、「サ」は運転台もモーターもない車両（付随車）だ。
次が**車両設備**を表していて、「ロ」はグリーン車、「ハ」が普通車、「ネ」は**寝台車**（「ネ」は寝るのネなのだ！）、食堂の「シ」が食堂車で「ユ」は郵便車、「ニ」は荷物車といった具合。「ロネ」がA寝台車というように組み合わさっている場合もある。

続く3ケタの数字は、百の位が電気方式を表す。「1

鉄ちゃんのギモン ● **Problems with Trains**

What do the serial numbers on train cars represent?

Don't worry, even if you've asked yourself this question, it doesn't make you a **train maniac**. But we all see serial numbers like "*ku-ha*-111" printed on the sides of train cars. (The "*ku*," "*ha*," etc. are written in katakana.) What do these represent?

JR informs us that these serial numbers basically use "a katakana notation plus 3 numeric digits" to represent the type of train car.

The first katakana indicates the presence of an **operator's seat** or motor in the car. "*Ku*" indicates a car with operator's controls (a control car), and "*mo*" indicates the presence of a motor in the car (a mid-motor car). So "*ku-mo*" indicates a car equipped with both operator's controls and a motor on board (a control motor car).

The next katakana indicates the **passenger facilities** the car is equipped with. "*Ro*" indicates a "green car" (first class); "*ha*" for regular cars; "*ne*" for **sleeper cars** (the "*ne*" actually stands for *neru*—"to sleep" in Japanese); "*shi*" for a dining car; "*yu*" for a postal transport car; and "*ni*" for baggage cars. These can be combined, so that "*ro-ne*" indicates a first-class sleeper car.

Next for the numbers ... The first digit indicates the kind

〜3」が直流電車、「4〜6」が直交流で、「7、8」は交流だ。

　十の位は電車の使用用途。「0」が**通勤型**、「1、2」が近郊型、「5〜7」が急行、「8」は特急、そして「9」は試作車とのこと。一の位は原則として製造された順番だ。例えば「231」なら「23」という系列の最初の型ということ。数字が大きいほど設計が新しいワケ。

　その後にハイフンを付けて各車両の**固有番号**が続いている。最近のJR東日本の電車は、「クハE455」など記号の後に「E」がついていることがあるが、これは「East」の頭文字。

　これだけ覚えておけば、子どもに尋ねられても大丈夫!?　ちなみに新幹線は数字だけで表している。最初の数字が「1」なら100系、「2」なら200系だ。

「クハ」は「運転台がある普通車」の意味
"Ku-ha" stands for a regular car with an operator's seat.

of electricity the train uses: 1 to 3 for DC, 4 to 6 for AC/DC, and 7 and 8 for AC.

The second digit indicates what the train is used for: 0 for **commuter trains**, 1 and 2 for trains connecting the surrounding provinces, 5 to 7 for express trains, 8 for super-express, and 9 for cars in test production. The third digit increases with consecutive design changes to the car. So if you see "231" after the katakana, you know it was the first design of the "23" built. The higher the third digit, the newer the car is.

This "prefix" is followed by a hyphen along with the car's **serial number**. Recently, JR East also includes an "E" (for "East") in the prefix, for example "*ku-ha*-E-455."

So if you can remember all of this, you should be safe when your children ask you. Also don't forget that the system is different for the shinkansen, using only numerals. If the number begins with "1" then it's a 100-series train; "2" for 200-series trains; etc.

終電後の駅員は
どうやって帰るのか？

終電が出てしまったら電車では帰れない。まるで**禅問答**だが、終電後の**駅員**はどうやって帰っているのか？

「実は、帰らないんですよ。交通機関がないので、終電後の帰宅も、始発前の出勤も無理。終電後に仮眠をとって始発に備えます」（京成電鉄広報）

どの鉄道会社でも、**おおむね**同じ答え。終電後の駅員は、片付けや安全確認をして、出入り口のシャッターを下ろす。売上金をしまい、券売機や架線の電源も落とす。30分〜1時間かかる作業だ。終電後も意外と忙しいのだ。始発前には、**逆の手順**を繰り返す。

「乗務員や**車掌**は、車庫の**仮泊所**に泊まるか、ホームに列車を止めたまま終着駅に泊まります。翌朝はまた、その駅からスタートです」（東京都交通局電車部）

鉄ちゃんのギモン ● Problems with Trains

How do train station employees get home after the last train has left?

After the last train of the night has gone, there's no way to get home. So the question may sound like a **Zen koan**, but how do **station employees** get home after the last train has gone?

Public relations of Keisei Electric Railway Co., Ltd., informs us: "After the last train, no one goes home at all. How could they? Since there's no public transportation available, leaving work after the last train, as well as coming in to work before the first train, is impossible. After the last train, train staff rest and get ready for the next morning."

The answer was **more or less** the same at all the rail companies we checked with. The station staff's duties after the departure of the last train include cleaning up, safety checks, closing the shutters of the station entrances, locking away the day's ticket sales, and shutting down the power for the ticket machines and the **track power lines**, all of which takes from 30 minutes to an hour. They're busier than you might have expected after the last train. Before the first train comes in the morning, they go through the same **procedure in reverse**.

"**Conductors** and train staff sleep in **break rooms** in the train garages, or simply park the train at the station they'll be starting from in the morning and sleep there," the rail division of the Tokyo Transportation Bureau told us.

都営地下鉄線の駅員は、朝9時〜翌朝9時の**24時間勤務**。その中で、時間をずらしながら夜間に仮眠をとる。安全管理上、乗務員の睡眠は仕事の一部。しかし駅員の場合は、そうも言っていられない。終電後に架線の工事・点検、構内での訓練などがあれば、仮眠時間が削られるそうだ。

　「駅員の仮眠室には直通の**インターホン**があり、何かあれば起こされます。緊急時に対応できるよう、休憩も食事も駅構内で済ませます」（東京都交通局五反田駅務区長）

　「終電後にコインロッカーの**荷物**を出したいというお客さまも、ときどき来ます。一人で処理できることであれば、係員は起こさず、**助役**一人で対処します。線内で**水漏れ**などトラブルがあれば、管制センターからの連絡で助役が起こされます。仮眠時間でもリラックスはできません」（同駅務区長）

　終電後の駅員の仕事は、思いのほか過酷な様子。お疲れさまです。

「終電」で帰るわけにもいかないし……？
Station staff look on as the rest of the world goes home.

鉄ちゃんのギモン ● Problems with Trains

Employees of the Metropolitan Subway work on **24-hour shifts**, from 9 AM to 9 AM the following morning. Over the course of one shift, they get to rest during breaks they take in rotation as well as while the station is closed. For conductors and train staff, getting enough rest is just one part of their job, for obvious safety reasons. But the same cannot be said of ordinary station staff, who sometimes have to cut back on rest time on account of maintenance or inspections of the power lines, or training and drills. "The break rooms for station staff are equipped with **intercoms**, and if a situation arises in which they are needed during their breaks, we wake them up. Breaks and meals all have to be taken inside the station to ensure we have full manpower in case of an emergency," the station service manager for Gotanda Station told us.

"Sometimes there are passengers who want to get their **belongings** out of the coin lockers even after the last train. If it's something one person can handle alone, the **assistant stationmaster** usually takes care of it without waking the attendants up. And when it rains, if there are **leaks** in the tunnels, the assistant stationmaster gets woken up by the control center. Even during break time, it's hard to relax," the station service manager told us. So the station attendant's work after the last train leaves is much harder than you might have expected. Good work! And good night!

新幹線の乗車率は
どうやって調べているのか？

お盆休みなどの帰省ラッシュ。道路の渋滞情報とあわせて、新幹線の**乗車率**もニュース報道されるが、新幹線のホームが帰省客であふれているニュース映像は、もはや**毎年恒例**だ。

テレビのニュースでは「新幹線の乗車率130％」「150％を超えた」などと伝えているが、この「乗車率」はどうやって計測しているのだろうか。

「乗車率は、**定員**に対して実際の乗車客が何人だったかで割り出しています。新幹線の場合、定員は座席数。つまり乗車客の数を座席数で割った数値を乗車率として発表しています」（JR東海広報室）

空席がひとつもなく立っている客もいない状態が「乗車率100％」ということだ。しかし、数ある新幹線の中でも東海道新幹線はとりわけ帰省ラッシュの混雑が激しいはず。乗客の実数はどうやって数えているのだろう。

カウント法を尋ねたところ、「**車掌**が各車両をまわって数えています」（同広報室）とのこと。

鉄ちゃんのギモン ● Problems with Trains

How do they calculate passenger boarding rates on the shinkansen?

During the Obon holidays when the city dwellers return to their hometowns, the news reports not only traffic jams on the highways, but also the "**passenger boarding rate**" on the shinkansen. Images on the news of station platforms crowded with passengers trying to make their way to their ancestral homes have become an **annual tradition**.

For example, we often hear reports reading, "The shinkansen is running at 130% of capacity" or "boarding rates in excess of 150%." But how do they calculate these figures?

According to Central Japan Railway Company's press office, "Boarding rates express the total number of passengers as a percentage of the train's **official capacity**. For the shinkansen, capacity is defined as the number of seats. So what we announce as the boarding rate is basically the number of passengers divided by the number of seats on the train."

So if every seat on the train is filled, and there's nobody standing, then you have a boarding rate of 100%. But of all the shinkansen lines, the Tokaido Shinkansen is particularly subject to crowding during the holidays. So how do they keep track of the numbers?

"The **conductor** counts as he makes his way through the train," JR Central confessed.

手にカウンターを持っているわけではなさそうだが、正確に計測できるものだろうか。
「新幹線では切符を拝見いたしますので、そのときに数えております」（同広報室）
　なんとも原始的な手法に頼っているものだ。

新幹線のホームに並ぶビジネスマン

Traveling businessmen line up for Shinkansen departure.

So are these figures reliable? It's hard to imagine the conductor walking through the train with a counter in his hand.

"On the shinkansen, all passengers' tickets are checked, so that's how the conductor makes his count," JR Central retorts. Not exactly the high-tech answer we were expecting.

Part 4

生活のギモン
Problems with Daily Life

氷屋の氷と家庭の氷はどこが違うのか？

夏になると冷たい飲み物が欲しくなる。氷をたっぷり入れてゴクゴクやりたいものだ。

ところで氷というのは昔からの氷屋の氷と家庭の冷蔵庫や**製氷機**でできるのとは違うらしい。どこが、どう違うのだろうか？

随分と数は減ったが、氷屋の**店頭**で鋸(のこぎり)で切っている音を聞くと何やら涼感を覚える。氷屋さんに「製氷機で作る氷とどこが違うの」と聞いた。

「味も持ちも全然違いますよ」と言うが、その理由はわからない。そこで、製氷会社を紹介してもらって問い合わせた。

「**まずは製氷の温度が違います**」と担当者。製氷機や冷蔵庫はマイナス15℃から20℃で1、2時間で作る。この方法だと表面に白い部分ができるが、ここに**不純物**が集まり、解けやすいのだという。これに対して製氷会社はなんと72時間もかけて氷を作る。原料は**水道水**だが、まずフィルターを通し、次いで「活

日本の生活のギモン ● Problems with Daily Life

Is there any difference between ice you get at an ice shop and ice you make at home?

What can beat something icy-cold to drink on a hot summer day? A tall glass filled with ice and your favorite beverage, and "gulp, gulp . . ." But it seems that the ice we used to get from the ice shop in the days of old is not quite the same as the ice we make nowadays in our freezers or that comes out of the **ice dispensers** at home. What's the difference?

These days, ice shops have dropped drastically in number, but some of us can still remember the cool sound of them cutting the ice with saws in their **storefronts**. We were able to find an ice shop nearby and decided to go in and ask some questions.

"The taste and resistance to melting are totally different," the man told us. But he wasn't able to give us much of an explanation as to the reason, so we had him introduce us to the manufacturer which supplies his ice, and went there to ask.

"**First of all**, the freezing temperature is different," we learned. Freezers and ice dispensers make ice at a temperature of –15 to –20°C and take about an hour or two for the ice to completely freeze. This method of freezing allows **impurities** to collect in the whitish area of the surface of the ice, and makes it easier for the ice to melt. On the other hand, ice

性炭ろ過機」にかけて不純物を取り除く。その水を缶に入れてかき混ぜ、空気を入れながら長い時間をかけて固めていくのだ。

「**カルキ**や**塩素**が取り除かれていますし、もっとも良い氷ができるマイナス10℃くらいでジックリ作るので硬い氷ができるのです」と製氷会社では言う。

こうして作ったものを150キロくらいの単位で氷屋に配送する。氷屋さんは言う。

「料金を払うのは135キロ分です。解けたり、鋸で切るときにロスが出るので、その分が差し引かれています」

なるほど、水道水を使って氷を作っているのに3.75キロ（1貫目）で450円もすると聞いて「高い」と思っていたが、こんなに手間をかけ、氷屋への物流費や店での人件費などを考えれば**仕方がない**値段か。氷屋さんは言った。

「昔は面白いようにもうかりましたが、今は製氷機が普及していますからね。味が違うことは間違いないのですが、昔のようにはいきません」

時代の変化と後継者難で氷屋は激減しているが、**決してなくならない**商売だろう。

manufacturers spend 72 hours making their ice. The water they use is ordinary **tap water**, but it passes through a water filter as well as an activated-carbon filtration system to remove any impurities. Then the water is poured into large cans where it is mixed to put air into it and slowly frozen.

"The ice is free of **chlorine** and **chlorides**, and we freeze it at the ideal temperature of –10 ºC, so it's much harder than the ice you make at home," says the ice manufacturer.

The ice which is sold to ice shops comes in blocks weighing about 150 kg. But "we sell it to the ice shops as 135 kg to account for melting during transport and weight lost during sawing."

When we first heard that they use ordinary tap water, we thought ¥450 for a 3.75 kg block of ice sounded a little expensive, but when you consider the time the manufacturer takes making the ice and the transport costs as well as the costs of the ice shop, **it doesn't seem too unreasonable**.

"In the old days, business was so good it was laughable," the ice shop owner told us. "But nowadays more and more people have ice dispensers in their refrigerators at home. Of course, the ice we sell tastes better, but it just doesn't sell like it used to."

As times change and fewer people are interested in continuing this line of business, things may be slower than they used to be, but the ice shop is still **by no means an endangered species**.

なぜコーヒーはスチール缶でビールはアルミ缶なのか？

飲料の缶にはスチール缶とアルミ缶があるが、コーヒー類がほとんどスチール缶なのに対して、ビールはアルミ缶だ。これには何か理由があるのか？

スチール缶とアルミ缶の違いは、触っただけでわかる。スチール缶は硬く、アルミ缶は軟らかい。飲み終えたビール缶は簡単につぶせるが、缶コーヒーは容易につぶせない。

「アルミ缶は熱伝導率が高いので、ビールを冷やすのに**適している**んです」と言うのはサッポロビール広報部だ。

「軽いので輸送コストも安い。リサイクル時に加工しやすいのも利点ですね。そのため、弊社で扱う飲料はほとんどがアルミ缶です」（同広報部）

空の缶を**持ち比べて**みると、たしかにアルミ缶のほうが軽い。

「ただ、アルミ缶は強度が弱いため、**炭酸飲料**のように内側から圧力がかかる液体を注入する必要があります。非炭酸の清涼飲料では耐衝撃性を実現できないので、強度の問題からスチール缶を使用していました。しかし最近は充填技術が発達して、お茶系の飲料にもアルミ缶が使われるようになっています」（キリンビバレッジ広報部）

日本の生活のギモン ● Problems with Daily Life

Why does coffee come in steel cans and beer in aluminum?

Beverage cans come in two types: steel and aluminum. Coffee is almost always in steel cans and beer in aluminum. Is there some reason for this?

It's easy to tell the difference between steel and aluminum. Steel cans are very hard, and it's difficult to put a dent in them with your bare hands, while aluminum cans are very soft and easy to crush.

"Aluminum conducts heat very will, so it's **ideal for** beer cans which need to be chilled," says Sapporo Beer's marketing department. "Also, aluminum's light weight helps us reduce shipping costs, and aluminum costs less to recycle. That's why we use aluminum cans for almost all the beverages we make."

It's easy to tell just by **hefting** two empty cans in your hands that aluminum is certainly lighter.

"However," Kirin Beverage tells us, "aluminum isn't very strong. This is fine for **carbonated beverages** which exert pressure from the inside against the can walls, but for non-carbonated liquids, aluminum doesn't provide enough protection against shock, so we use steel instead. But with advances in bottling technology, we're now able to use aluminum for tea beverages."

現在、同社のお茶系飲料はアルミ缶とスチール缶が半々だが、コーヒーは**全部が**スチール缶だという。
「技術的にはアルミ缶の使用も可能だが、イメージの問題」（同広報部）
とのこと。
　近ごろは、フタの開け閉めが可能な「ボトル缶」を見かけることも多い。
　従来はボトル缶といえばアルミ製だったが、スチール缶の加工、軽量化の研究も続けられ、スチール製のボトル缶も登場。
　ちなみに北九州の八幡製鉄所周辺ではスチール缶入りのビールも売られているそうだ。

Currently, they've switched to aluminum for about half of their tea products, but steel is still **exclusively** used for coffee beverages. "We have the technology to use aluminum for coffee too, but it just doesn't suit the image of the product."

Recently, "bottle cans" with screw-on caps have also appeared. Bottle cans have so far been made exclusively from aluminum, but advances in lighter-weight steel processing have made steel bottle cans also possible.

And if you're interested in drinking beer out of a steel can, it seems you can find some in the neighborhood of Yahata Iron & Steel Company in Kitakyushu.

代々木の「々」は何と読む?

同じ漢字を繰り返し表記するときに使う「々」。「代々木」と書いた場合は「よ」と読むが、これが佐々木だと「さ」になるし、云々ならば「ぬん」!? この「々」自体はいったい何と読むのか?

正々堂々、時々刻々、山々に人々——ふだんの生活でも「々」を使うことは多いが、漢和辞典の総画索引で引いても3画の項に記載がない。

「同じ漢字を繰り返すときに使う"々"は、漢字ではなく記号です。繰り返し記号には他にも"ゝ"や"く"などがありますが、それらすべてをまとめて"**踊り字**"と呼んでいます。記号ということで、漢字としては載せていないのでしょう」(文化庁文化部国語課)

踊り字という名称は、昭和21(1946)年に文部省が作成した「くりかへし符號の使ひ方(をどり字法)案」という文書に出てくる。これによると「々」は「仝」の字から転化したもの。「仝」は「同」の異体字だから、同文書では「々」を「同の字点」と呼んでいる。

日本の生活のギモン ● **Problems with Daily Life**

What's that "character" you use to repeat kanji called?

When the same kanji appears twice in a Japanese word, it is usually not written out the second time but is replaced by 々. In the place name Yoyogi (代々木) this is read "*yo*"; in the family name Sasaki (佐々木) it's read "*sa*"; and in the phrase *unnun* (云々) it's read *nun*. But what's this thing's actual name?

You see it all over the printed page in *seisei dodo* (**fair and square**, 正々堂々), *jiji kokukoku* (momentarily, 時々刻々), *yamayama-ni hitobito* (people in the mountains, 山々に人々), but you'll be hard pressed to find it listed anywhere in your kanji dictionary.

According to the language division of Japan's Agency for Cultural Affairs: "The symbol 々 we use to repeat kanji is just that: a symbol. It isn't a character and it isn't kanji. That's why it's not included in kanji dictionaries. It is one of what are known as "**iteration marks**" (*odori-ji*, lit. "dancing mark" in Japanese), just like ヽ, and is used to repeat hiragana."

The word *odori-ji* can be found in the Ministry of Education's "Scheme for the Use of Repetition Marks (Dancing Marks)" of 1946. This states that 々 evolved from 仝, a glyph of the kanji *do* 同 (English "same"), and refers to 々 by the name *do-no jiten* (lit. do mark). Likewise, ヽ is used to repeat

同様に、ひらがなを繰り返すときに使う「ゝ」は「一つ点」、「く」を縦にのばしたような形で2文字以上繰り返す記号は「くの字点」などと呼ぶが、あくまで呼び名であって読み方ではないそうだ。
　「々」は出版・印刷業界では「ノマ点」と呼ばれることもある。カタカナの「ノ」と「マ」を合わせたような記号だからだ。しかし、一部のワープロを除いて、「ノマ」でも「同の字」でも「々」は出てこない。では、どうすればいいか。
　「おなじ」「くりかえし」「どう」などと打って変換キーを押すと、繰り返し記号が出てくるはずだ。覚えておいて損はないゾ!

single hiragana and is referred to as *hito-tsu-ten* (lit. "single mark"), but these are just "names" for these symbols and do not indicate how they are to be read in context.

In the printing industry, 々 is referred to as a *no-ma-ten* (lit. "*no-ma* mark") because of its resemblance to a combination of the katakana for *no* (ノ) and *ma* (マ). This symbol can also be accessed on some word processors by typing *no-ma* or *do no ji*.

But even though this symbol doesn't have one definite name, maybe it's better that we have a few choices anyhow. If you can remember at least one of the names, you should have no trouble getting it to display on your computer.

なぜ男物と女物のシャツは打ち合わせが逆？

　和服の場合は男も女も同じで、**通常は右前**に着る。しかし洋服は男物が右前なのに女物は左前と決まっている。どうして打ち合わせ方が違うのか。

　「右前」「左前」という呼び方はややこしいが、和服を着るときに右の身頃を先（前）に着付けるのが右前。右手がすっと**懐**に入る合わせ方だ。左前は死に装束で忌み嫌われている。

　洋服は右側にボタンが付いていて、左側のボタンホールをくぐらせて留めるのが右前。人類の9割は**右利き**だから、右前のほうが着やすいというのが定説だ。
　『西洋服飾史』（丹野郁編／東京堂出版）によれば、前開きでボタン留めの服はアジアに起源があり、**十字軍**を経てヨーロッパに伝わったのは13世紀ごろ。次第にヨーロッパの男性服として定着していった。

Why do men's and women's shirts button up on different sides?

With traditional Japanese clothing, both men and women wear their robes the same way, **with the left part of the robe over the right**. But with Western clothing, men's shirts button up left over right while women's shirts button up right over left. What's the reason for putting the buttons on different sides of the shirt?

In Japanese, these two ways of wearing clothes are called *migi-mae* and *hidari-mae*. The usual way of wearing Japanese robes is *migi-mae*, where the right (*migi*) hand side is wrapped around the body first (*mae*, lit. "before"). This way makes it easy to use your right hand to reach into the **fold** of the robe. *Hidari-mae* (left first) is only used in dressing the dead for a funeral.

For Western clothes, *migi-mae* equates to having the buttons on the right side of the shirt, and the button holes on the left. Since 90% of the world's population is supposed to be **right-handed**, this way is considered easier to wear.

According to *A History of Western Dress* (edited by Kaoru Tanno), front-opening garments closed together with buttons have their roots in Asia, and were brought back to Europe by **crusaders** during the 13th century. Eventually, this became the button-up shirt and the standard for men's clothing in

婦人服への普及はもう少し後れるが、最初のうちは男と同じ右前だったようだ。それがいつしか婦人服だけが左前に変わってしまった。

　「当時、女性はまだコルセットを身につけていて、洋服をひとりで着ることは少なかった。特に高貴な身分の女性は召し使いに着せてもらっていたため、向かい合った召し使いが着せやすいように打ち合わせが逆になったという説が有力ですが、**はっきりしたことはわかっていません**」(服装史学者)

　他にも左前は**授乳**に便利だからという説や、女性の地位が低かった時代は男性と同じ洋服を身につけることに社会的な抵抗があって打ち合わせが逆になったという説、女性の地位向上が叫ばれた19世紀になって女性側から差異化を求めたという説など諸説が入り乱れているのが現状だ。
　中には「左前のほうが脱がせやすいから」なんてスケベな説もある。本書としてはこの説に１票!?

写真は右前の男物
Migi-mae, or
left-over-right.

Europe.

It took a while for the same trend to catch on with women, but it seems that at first, women's shirts also buttoned up left-over-right. So how did only women's clothing get changed to right-over-left?

According to a fashion historian we asked, "In those days women still wore corsets and it was rare for a woman to be able to dress herself. Most women of the aristocracy had servants to help them dress. While **there is no single authoritative answer on the question**, it seems most likely that the buttons were switched to the left side to make it easier for the servant to button her mistress up."

Other theories include: Right-over-left is more convenient for **breast-feeding**... Since women's social rank was lower than that of men, there was resistance to women wearing the same clothing... Women demanded "their own" shirts as calls were made for improvement of women's status during the 19th century... etc. etc.

There's even one sexual theory behind this: that women's shirts buttoning up right-over-left makes it easier for a man to remove a woman's clothing. Now if that isn't convincing...

「なるべくお早めにお召し上がりください」とは何日？

　食品が時間経過とともに**傷んでくる**のは自然の道理。生モノはもちろん、ハムやチーズ、納豆などの加工食品も、封を切った後は気になるところだ。

　そうした加工食品の多くには、「開封後はなるべくお早めにお召し上がりください」と表示されているが、「なるべくお早めに」って、具体的にはどれくらいの日数なのか。

　食品には、食品衛生法などの定めにより、食品名、製造者名、原材料名、使用添加物名、内容量、使用期限、保存方法、使用の注意などの**表示**が義務付けられている。**遺伝子組み換え食品**と**アレルギー物質**を含む食品についての表示も義務化された。

　使用期限には、「**消費期限**」と「**賞味期限**」の2種類があり、いずれも開封前の期限のこと。

　消費期限は弁当や**総菜**、食肉など品質が急速に劣化しやすい食品について、「定められた方法で保存すれば衛生上の危害が発生しない」と認められる年月日のこと。おおむね5日以内とされる。

"Consume quickly." Could you be more specific?

It's the law of nature that food **goes bad** with the passing of time. It's a given with unprocessed foods, of course; but even with processed foods like ham, cheese, or *natto*, once you open the package, it's a race against the clock.

Many of these foods bear the labeling "Please Consume Quickly after Opening." But just how quick is "Quickly?"

As specified by the Food Hygiene Act, **labeling** must indicate the food's name, ingredients, additives, manufacturer's name, product weight, expiration date, storage instructions, and any warnings etc. **Genetically altered foods** as well as foods containing **allergens** also now have to be clearly labeled.

There are two kinds of expiration date: a "**limit for consumption**" and a "**limit for best quality**"; but both of these are decided before the products even reach the market shelves, regardless of when you open the package.

The "limit for consumption" is used for boxed bento-lunches, **pre-made side dishes**, uncooked meat and other foods which are subject to a rapid decline in quality after processing. This date represents "the date up to which the product may be consumed safely provided proper storage conditions

一方の賞味期限は、消費期限表示食品以外の食品について、「定められた**保存方法**によれば品質の保持が十分に可能」と認められる年月日のこと。製造・加工の日から３カ月を超えるものは年月のみの表示でよい。
　さて、本題の「開封後はお早めに」の目安だが、厚生労働省によれば、具体的な日数は法的に決められてはいないとのこと。
　そこで、「お早め表示」のある食品をいくつか選び、メーカーに直接聞いてみたところ、やはり食品ごとに違うようだ。

　目安としては、ヨーグルト、ハムは開封後２、３日以内、カップデザートは３日以内、**ザーサイ**は３、４日以内、ナチュラルチーズは７日以内、プロセスチーズは10日以内、塩辛は開封前の賞味期限（３カ月）と同じ。
　ただし、いずれも**ラップ**をしての**冷蔵保存**が原則。メーカーによって日数が異なる場合もあり、これらはあくまでも品質保持の**目安**でしかない。

　過ぎたら腐ってしまうというリミットではないが、逆に、それ以内なら絶対腐らないという保証でもないのだ。

are maintained," usually within five days of processing.

For other food products, the "limit of best quality" is used to indicate the date up until which "quality can be sufficiently maintained, given appropriate **storage conditions**." If this period is longer than 3 months from the date of manufacture or processing, only the month and the year are indicated.

Back then to our original question of what exactly is meant by "Quickly After Opening." According to the Ministry of Health, Labour and Welfare, there is no legal definition of what is meant by "Quickly." So we selected a few products with this "Quickly" labeling and tried asking the manufacturers directly. As you might suspect, we got a wide range of answers.

As a rough guide: for yogurt and ham, two to three days after opening; for pudding and other cup desserts, three days; *zha cai*, three to four days, fruit juice, seven days; processed cheese, ten days; and for *shiokara*, it's the same as the "limit of best quality" (usually around three months).

Furthermore, all of the above assume **storage in a refrigerator** and **plastic wrapping**. Also, the definition of "Quality" can vary with the manufacturer, so these are only **guidelines** at best.

It would seem then that while the "limit of best quality" is not exactly a warning of when the product will go bad, neither is it a promise of until when the product will be absolutely "good."

洋服の「フリーサイズ」とは、どういう基準?

洋服のサイズは一般的にS、M、Lなどに分かれているが、「**フリーサイズ**」「**F**」と表示された衣料をたまに見かける。

これはいったいどういう大きさのものなのか。「フリー」というからには、Sの人もLの人も着られるのだろうか。

まずは洋服のサイズを管轄する経済産業省の製造産業局繊維課に問い合わせてみた。

「国内の**既製衣料品**のサイズは日本工業規格(JIS)で決められていますが、JISには『フリーサイズ』という規定はありません。衣料品のサイズの規格は、表示が法令で義務づけられた規格ではありませんが、消費者への情報提供の観点から、なるべくJISに沿ったサイズ表示にすることを推奨します」

大手衣料メーカー各社に尋ねたところ、「JIS規格にのっとって製造しているのでフリーサイズは扱っていない」という答えがほとんど。靴下やベルトにかぎり、フリーサイズと表示する場合もあるが、これは、伸縮性があったりサイズ調節が可能で、たいていの人が使えるためだ。

Exactly what size is "one-size-fits-all?"

The usual sizes for clothing are "S," "M," and "L," but once in a while you come across "F" for *furi saizu* (**one-size-fits-all**, or Japanese "free size.") But is that really a "size"? Is it really going to fit someone who wears a small AND someone who wears a large?

First, we tried inquiring with the textile department of the Ministry of Economy, Trade and Industry (METI)'s Manufacturing Industries Bureau, which has jurisdiction over clothing sizes. "Sizes for domestic **ready-made clothing** are regulated by the Japanese Industrial Standards (JIS), but the JIS make no mention of 'one-size-fits-all.' Standards for clothing sizes are not legally binding on the manufacturers, but from the point of view of providing accurate information to consumers, we recommend **adherence to** JIS-established size markings."

We asked around with a couple of major clothing manufacturers, but the answer was almost always the same: "We follow the JIS, so we don't have any one-size-fits-all." Belts and socks were the only items we found whose manufacturers used the term "one-size-fits-all," but these are understandable cases.

しかし、実際にはフリーサイズ表示の衣料品が少なくない。なぜか。業界関係者が打ち明ける。

　「ノベルティーや**土産物**のTシャツはフリーサイズが一番売れる。だれでも着られそうだから、人にも贈りやすいしね。ワイシャツと違って、Tシャツはサイズがきっちり合わなくても着られるから、男物はL、女物はMをフリーサイズ表示にして出荷することが多い」（カジュアル衣料専門の卸問屋）

　男物の場合、Lサイズで男性の9割近くをカバーできるそうだ。

　「フィット性を重視しないカジュアル衣料は、ワンサイズ展開しかないものもあり、その場合フリーサイズと表示される。これはあくまでたいていの人が"入る"という意味で、体形に合っているかは別問題。太った人とやせた人では、当然着たときのラインが変わってきます」（男性ファッション誌のスタイリスト）

　見栄えを重視するなら、なるべく**試着**してみたほうがよさそうだ。

But in reality, one-size-fits-all clothing is not uncommon at all. We were able to find a casual clothes retailer familiar with the industry who could fill us in on the story. "Novelty and **souvenir** T-shirts sell better when labeled 'one-size-fits-all.' It gives the impression that anyone will be able to wear them, so it makes it easier to buy them as gifts for others. Unlike dress shirts, T-shirts don't have to fit perfectly to be wearable, so what is manufactured as a men's 'L' or a women's 'M' often gets shipped out labeled as 'one-size-fits-all.'" It turns out that around 90% of men find no problem with wearing a size "L" T-shirt.

A stylist for a men's fashion magazine told us, "With casual clothes, where a perfect fit isn't that important, a lot of clothes only come in one size, so the 'one-size-fits-all' labeling is the only natural choice. But all this really tells us is that the article is 'wearable' for the average person. Of course, the way it fits the body will be a little different for each kind of body type."

Anyhow, if you're worried about a perfect fit, we recommend **trying** it **on** before you buy.

「1万円入りま〜す」の意味は?

ファストフードなどの支払いで1万円札を出すと、店員が「1万円入りま〜す」と掛け声を出すのは何のため?

客には別に「1万円お預かりします」と言うので、他の店員に伝えるためと思われるが、中には店員がその声に全く反応しない店もある。レジに入った札の数を細かくチェックしているわけではなさそうだ。

5000円札と1万円札の時は「入ります」の声を出し、他の店員は「お願いします」と答えるよう指導しているというドトールコーヒーの話。

「主に3つの意味があります。まず、高額紙幣を受け取ったことを他の店員に伝えることで、**釣り銭**の渡し間違いがより起きにくくなります。また、レジ係が紙幣を**着服する**のを防止する意味もあります。最後が、客の釣り銭詐欺を防ぐためです」(広報担当)

"¥10,000 going in!"
Do you have to tell the world?

In fast food restaurants and the like, when you hand the cashier a ¥10,000 bill, they call out as if to let the whole shop know, "¥10,000 going in!" But why? They always verbally confirm the amount with the customer before actually taking the money. So if not for the customer's sake, is this to let the other employees know about the ¥10,000 bill? Yet it doesn't seem that they should be concerned with the number of bills going into the **till**. There are shops where the other employees pay no attention whatsoever to the cashier's "¥10,000" cry.

Doutor Coffee trains its employees to make this kind of announcement whenever they receive a ¥5,000 or ¥10,000 bill at the register, and for all other employees on the floor to make a verbal acknowledgement of the announcement. So if you pay with a ¥10,000 bill the cashier will call out "¥10,000 coming in" and the other employees will say "alright."

According to Doutor's press office, "There are three main reasons. Firstly, making other employees aware of the large bill makes it less likely for the cashier to make mistakes in giving the customer his **change**. Next, it helps prevent the cashier from **pocketing** the bill. Finally, it helps prevent customers from trying to get more change than they're entitled to by trying to argue about how much money they gave the cashier."

釣り銭詐欺防止とは意外だが、1000円札などを出しておきながら、後で「1万円札を出したじゃないか」などと難癖をつけて、釣り銭を詐取しようとするヤカラが結構いるというのだ。
　どの店も**高額紙幣**の対応には苦労しているようで、1万円札を腰のポーチにしまって代わりに1000円札の束を出す"セルフ両替方式"の店もあれば、他の店員に実際に紙幣を見せて確認するファーストキッチンなど、方法はさまざまだ。

　中でも厳しいのが吉野家。高額紙幣は店の奥の責任者に渡し、両替してもらうシステムになっている。
　「両替行為を挟むことで、より釣り銭間違いを防止することができます。また、高額紙幣をレジに置かないことが、強盗などの犯罪を少なくすることにつながります」（広報・IR担当）

　なお、マクドナルドは「マニュアルに"高額紙幣は確認する"とありますが、"1万円入ります"の掛け声は特に**義務**付けておりません」（広報担当）とのことだ。

You might not have expected this to be necessary to stop fraudulent customers, but there are actually folks who knowingly hand the casheir ¥1,000 and then say "Wait a minute! That was ¥10,000 I gave you!"

It seems that all shops worry about how their employees handle **large bills**. For example, employees at some shops keep pouches at their waists with ¥10,000 bundles of ¥1,000 bills for the express purpose of changing ¥10,000 bills before putting the money into the register—a system they call "self-exchange." At First Kitchen, another fast food chain, employees are trained not only to make an announcement, but to hold the bill up for other employees to see before putting it in the register.

Yoshinoya seems to have taken a particularly strict approach. When the cashier gets a large bill, it has to be taken to the back of the shop to be changed by the manager before any money can be put in the till. "By keeping tight control on the exchange of bills, we're better able to prevent mistakes when giving customers their change. Also, the fact that we don't keep any large bills in the register makes us less of a target for robbers," says Yoshinoya's press office.

And according to McDonald's, "Our training manual instructs employees to 'verify large bills,' but there's no **obligation** to announce, *ichi man-en hairimasu*!"

コンドーム自動販売機が銭湯の隣にあるのはなぜ？

恥ずかしながら、記者はSEXが大好きである。女房への週1回のオツトメはもちろん、若い娘との火遊びにも精を出す身としてコンドームは必需品。ところで、なぜか「明るい家族計画」でおなじみの専用自販機は、**銭湯**の隣に設置されていることが多い。

都内の銭湯を統括する東京都公衆浴場業生活衛生同業組合にそのワケをたずねると、

「ちょっとわかりませんねぇ……」とのこと。

そこで、**避妊具メーカー**に尋ねてみた。「銭湯の近くに**薬局**があった頃の**名残**でしょう」と言うのはメーカー最大手のオカモトだ。

「1999年まで、避妊具の自販機の設置には保健所の認可が必要でした。コンドームは**医療用具**なので薬局の前に認可がおりやすく、頻繁に設置されました。自販機は薬局の営業が終わってから稼動する。そのため、夜遅く銭湯の帰りに気軽に買える自販機はよく売れたからでしょう」（オカモト広報部）

時代は流れ、かつての**個人経営**の薬局がスーパーなどに店変わりする中、コンドームの自販機は風雪

日本の生活のギモン ● Problems with Daily Life

Why are there condom vending machines next to public bathhouses?

While it's a bit embarrassing, this writer has to admit to loving sex. Whether it's the "once-a-week" with my wife or a little adventure with the younger ladies, condoms are one of the necessities of life. But have you ever wondered why you often see condom vending machines, with their familiar slogan—"Happy Family Planning"—right nextdoor to **public bathhouses**? When we tried asking someone from the Tokyo Sento Association, which oversees all public bathhouses in the metropolis, the answer was, "Hmmm . . . I don't know."

An inquiry with a **contraceptive manufacturer** proved a little more instructive. "It a **relic** of the days when every public bath used to have a **pharmacy** nearby," was the answer from industry leader Okamoto. "Until 1999, permission from the local health office was required to set up a condom vending machine. Since condoms are technically considered **medical devices**, it was always easiest to get permission to set them up in front of pharmacies. And the vending machines remained in operation even after the pharmacies would close for the day. This made them popular with people making their way home from the *sento* late at night."

Even as times change, and the old **mom-and-pop** pharmacies of the past get replaced by supermarkets, the condom

に耐え銭湯とともに残ったというわけだ。ところで、昨今はコンビニでも手軽にコンドームを買うことができるのに、なぜ自販機が撤去されずに残っているのだろう？

「理由の1つが売り上げの多さです。国内で生産される年間約6億個（そのうち約2％が輸出品。国内向けより約1〜2センチ長い）のうち、3億個以上が自販機で買われています」（ある自販機の調査・設置会社）

現在も設置されているのは、対面販売を恥ずかしがる人が多いことと、その夜の実戦用に買う人が多いためだという。

vending machines, along with the bathhouses, seem to have stood the test of time. But nowadays, you can buy condoms in any convenience store, so why keep the vending machines around?

"One reason for keeping them is that they're still making money. Of the approximately 600 million condoms produced domestically a year (2% is for export, and manufactured 1 to 2 cm longer than for the Japanese market), over 300 million are purchased from vending machines," says a firm specializing in vending machine research.

The enduring popularity of these vending machines shows that people are still maybe a little embarrassed to buy their condoms from someone at a cash register, and perhaps also that there are a lot more people who consider it wise to buy them on their way home then we may expect.

理美容院で切り落とした髪の毛はその後どうなるのか？

理美容院で毎日のように切られる髪を集めれば相当な量になるはず。何かに再利用されたりしているのだろうか。

「切った髪は捨てるしかありませんね。40〜50年ほど前までは、髪を回収したり買い取ってくれる業者もありましたが、今はほとんどなくなってしまいました」（理容業界関係者）

もともと人毛には、カツラや付け毛、理美容師の練習・試験用マネキンの材料のほか、薬品の原料にするという用途もある。

人毛からは、パーマ液などに使われるアミノ酸系物質「L-システイン」を抽出することができるのだ。

短く切った髪でも薬品の原料にできるため、製薬会社と理容組合がタイアップして髪を回収したことがあったという。

「人毛の需要はあるのですが、現在は回収を行っていません。日本で調達するとコストがかかりすぎるので、中国からの輸入に頼っているんです。中国の人毛は、安い上に黒くて太いストレートヘアなので、カツラにも薬品にも最適。日本人の髪は脱色などによる傷みも激しく、メーカーにとって魅力的ではあ

What happens to all the hair that gets cut at the hairdresser's?

Can you imagine the hairball a hairdresser could **put together** just from what gets swept from the floor in a day's work? If only there were some way to put all this hair to good use!

A friend in the know in the world of hairdressing sadly informs us, "Unfortunately, it's good for little more than filling garbage cans. Forty or 50 years ago hairdressers were able to sell the cut hair, but nowadays there's hardly anyone left who will buy it."

In the past, common uses for human hair included **wigs** and **extensions**, hairdressers' training mannequins, as well as **pharmaceutical applications**.

Also the amino acid L-cysteine used in permanent solution can be extracted from human hair.

In the past, pharmaceutical companies went as far as teaming up with hairdressers to get even the short-cut hair, but those days are long over.

"There still is a demand for human hair, but there's no point in collecting it anymore. In Japan, the cost of **procurement** is too high, so China is the main supplier. Chinese hair is black, thick, and straight—and cheap—making it **ideal** both for wig makers as well as pharmaceuticals. Recently, Japanese hair exhibits damage due to excessive dying, making it a less

りません」(業界関係者)
　ちなみに人毛は可燃ゴミ。「**燃えるゴミ**」の日にゴミ袋に入れて収集所に出しているそうだ。

昔は買い取る業者がいた
People actually used to buy this!

attractive raw material."

So what happens to the cut hair of Japan these days? It hits the sidewalk, in a garbage bag, right along with all the other **combustible trash**.

銀行や役所で なぜ「シヤチハタ」はダメ!?

銀行の口座開設や役所の届け出の際、印鑑は「シヤチハタ不可」と書かれていることが多い。なぜ?

まずは、みずほ銀行広報部の話。

「**印字面がゴムなので、何度も押すことで摩耗したり潰れたりで、印影が崩れる恐れがあります。インク式なので濃淡が一定じゃないという要素もあり、シヤチハタなどゴム印は受け付けておりません」

続いて東京23区のある区役所。

「そもそも印字面が変形しやすい**ゴム印**は、**印鑑**という認識は持っておりません。印鑑登録はできませんし、各種届け出などでも印鑑としては有効ではありません」(広報課)

え、印鑑じゃない!?

名指しされたシヤチハタはさぞくやしいだろう、と聞いてみたら、「実は私どもも公文書などで使う印鑑として作っている認識はありません」(総務部広報担当)と、何とも拍子抜けする答え。

「公文書用としての印鑑は各自治体ごとの条例で、同じ型で作っていない、変形しないなどの条件が定

Why can't "Shachihata" stamps be used at banks and public offices?

If you try to open a new bank account or to complete some official business at a **government office**, you'll often see "No Shachihata" next to the place for you to affix your personal seal. Why not?

First we tried asking public relations at Mizuho Bank. "There are a couple of reasons for not accepting Shachihatas. First of all, since they're rubber stamps, the **stamp surface** is subject to wear with repeated use. Also, the fact that they're self-inking means that the darkness of the ink changes over the course of use."

Next we inquired at a ward office in Tokyo. "Since the shape of rubber is easily altered, we don't recognize any **rubber stamp** for use as a **personal seal**. You can't register a Shachihata, and their use on any official document renders the instrument void."

What? You mean they're not actually seals after all?

So how do does Shachihata, Inc., the manufacturer of these convenient self-inking stamps, feel about having been singled out like this? "We don't intend these stamps to be used in lieu of personal seals on official documents either," their press office says ... They seem to be taking things in stride. "Local laws governing personal seals dictate that no two

められています。しかし、ゴム印は印字面がゴムという素材の性質上、常に同じ**印影**を再現できない。だから当社でも、あくまで社内書類などで使う事務印のカテゴリーで販売しています」(広報担当)

　以前は印影も時間が経つと**変色**したりしたが、今ではインクの改良で優に10年以上は同じ状態を保持できるようになった。**それでも**ゴム印である以上、**公文書**用としての条件をクリアするのは不可能なのだという。
　なお、シヤチハタ（ヤは大文字）は社名で、俗にシヤチハタと呼ばれるハンコの商品名は「Xスタンパー」。社名が"不可"とアチコチで名指しされる気分は？　と聞くと、「それだけ社名が浸透した証拠かな、と納得しています」(広報担当)と複雑な表情だった。

identical seals should be made, and that the shape of the seal must not be altered. Also, rubber stamps, by their very nature, can never be guaranteed to produce exactly the same **stamped image** every time. That's why we market these stamps as mere office supplies, intended at best for memos and other unofficial documents at work."

In the past, the stamped ink was subject to rapid **discoloration**; but with improvements to the ink, the imprinted image is resistant to fading for over 10 years. **Nonetheless**, the fact that the stamping surface is made of rubber disqualifies them from use on **official documents**.

And in case you didn't know, "Shachihata" is the name of the company, and the stamps, colloquially called by the company's name, are actually called "X Stampers," at least in the Shachihata catalog. But don't they feel like they've been singled out, seeing the negation of their company name any time you go to the bank or city hall? "No, not really . . . we just accept it as proof of the extent to which out company name has become part of Japanese culture." It seems they've learned to deal with their popularity (or lack thereof).

なぜ暮れに"第九"が演奏されるのか？

年末になると必ず聞こえてくるベートーベン交響曲第九番。第4楽章「歓喜の歌」の合唱を聴かないと年を越せないという人もいるだろうが、なぜ暮れに"第九"が演奏されるのか？

有力な説は2つある。1つ目は**意外や意外**、第2次大戦中の学徒出陣が絡む話だ。

昭和18（1943）年の学徒出陣の際、東京音楽学校（現・東京芸術大学）が壮行音楽会を開き、第九の第4楽章が演奏された。**器楽科**と**声楽科**の両方が**参加**できる、というのがその理由だ。

そして終戦後の昭和22（1947）年12月30日、戦死した学生を悼む音楽会が日比谷公会堂で開かれ、再び第九が選ばれた。以降も慰霊音楽会が行われ、年末の第九が**定着**していった——という物語だ。

感動的な話だが、残念ながら「そのような演奏会があったことを示す資料がない」（東京芸術大学音楽学部）「音楽会の記録は見つからない」（日比谷公会

日本の生活のギモン ● **Problems with Daily Life**

Why does it all end with Beethoven's Ninth?

Performances of the Ode to Joy from the 4th movement of **Beethoven's 9th symphony** are a year's end tradition, and many people even feel like they can't properly welcome in the new year without having been to a performance. But how did Beethoven become a Japanese New Year's tradition?

There are two main theories. The story behind the first theory begins rather **unexpectedly**, with the conscription of students into the military during WWII. At a concert given in 1943 by the Tokyo School of Music (currently the Tokyo University of Fine Arts) in honor of students who were being conscripted the following year, the "Ode to Joy" was included in the program, supposedly for the reason that both the **symphony** and the **choir** could **take part in** the performance.

And after that, on December 30 1947, another concert was held at Hibiya Auditorium dedicated to the memory of students fallen in the war, with Beethoven's 9th on the program once again. And as these kinds of concerts grew in popularity during the postwar years, performing Beethoven's 9th around the end of the year just seemed to **catch on**.

That's a **moving story**, but unfortunately, "Nothing in our records indicate that such a concert was ever held" (Music Department at Tokyo University of Fine Arts), and Hibiya

堂）ので、真偽は定かでない。

　もう1つは、NHK交響楽団（N響）の前身の日本交響楽団が始めた、という説。
「毎年師走に第九を演奏するようになったのは、昭和22年12月9〜13日の演奏会が最初です」（N響）
　その理由の1つに、楽団員のモチ代稼ぎがあったというから、これまた驚きだ。

「戦後間もないころ、楽団員は低収入で生活が苦しかった。そこで、合唱団もつく第九を演奏すれば、その家族や友人が大勢聴きにきてくれて臨時収入になるので年が越せる、というのです。その慣例が徐々に全国に広まり、アマの人も演奏や合唱に参加するようになって、年末＝第九の構図ができたのでしょう」（N響）

　ちなみに、日本で最初に第九を演奏したのは大正7（1918）年、徳島県の収容所にいたドイツ人捕虜。年末に第九を演奏するのは日本だけの風習とか。日本人は第九が大好きなのだ。

Auditorium also seems unable to find anything to prove the concerts actually took place. So it's hard to tell whether the story is true or not.

The other theory goes back to the former Nippon Symphony Philharmonic, currently the NHK Symphony, according to whom: "The tradition of performing Beethoven's 9th at year's end begins with concerts we held from December 9 to 13, 1947." One surprising reason for this choice of programming was to help the symphony members earn extra cash for the holidays.

"Shortly after the war, the musicians were very poorly paid and life was tough. So by programming music requiring a large number of performers, like Beethoven's 9th, they could be sure to get big audiences made up of the family and friends of those performing in both the symphony as well as in the choir. This gave them enough extra income to be able to celebrate New Year's. As this continued year after year, the "Ode to Joy" came to be accepted as part of end-of-the-year activities in Japan."

As trivia, Japan got its first performance of Beethoven's 9th in 1918, given by prisoners of war being held in Tokushima prefecture. It also seems that Japan is the only country with this year-end "Ode to Joy" tradition. Could Beethoven have ever imagined he'd become so popular half-way around the world in Japan?

Q ペットは何を飼ってもいいのか？

A

ニシキヘビにサソリ、ワニなど、物騒な動物の捕獲騒ぎをよく耳にする。こんな危険動物たちが"ペット"というのも変な話。ペットは何を飼ってもいいのだろうか？

「人に危害を加える恐れがある動物は『特定動物』として各都道府県ごとの条例で**指定されて**おり、十分な飼育**施設**をつくったうえで**知事**の許可を得ることになっています」（環境省動物愛護管理室）

つまり、ワシントン条約に抵触しないかぎり、象だろうが虎だろうが、許可さえ得れば飼うことが可能なのだ。

東京都の場合、ライオンなどの大型哺乳類、わしたか類、へび類など19区分が「特定動物」に指定されている。

例えば、毒ヘビを飼う場合には、フタ付きで施錠ができる**水槽**と**抗毒血清**を用意することが必須。実際には、個人で大型の「特定動物」を飼っている人は少ないというが、これらの動物が逃げ出した場合、

日本の生活のギモン ● **Problems with Daily Life**

Are you allowed to keep anything as a pet?

You sometimes hear sensational stories of terrible escaped "pets" being caught in the cities: **pythons**, scorpions, alligators, etc. These seem unnatural choices for household pets; but are there any restrictions on the kinds of animals you're allowed to keep?

According to the Animal Protection Office of the Ministry of the Environment, "Animals which pose a risk to humans are **classified** as 'controlled animals' in accordance with the laws of each prefecture. A prospective owner has to demonstrate the establishment of proper **facilities** to keep the animal and the permission of the **prefecture's governor** is required."

So basically, as long as it's not in violation of the Washington Convention, and as long as you can get the governor's permission, you could even have a "pet" elephant or tiger.

In Tokyo, there are 19 categories of "controlled animals," including large **mammals** (such as lions), eagles and hawks, and snakes, to name a few.

For example, if you want to keep a poisonous snake, you need to have an **aquarium** with a locking cover, and a supply of **antidote for the venom** on hand. Actually, cases of individuals keeping large "controlled animals" are rare, but in

すみやかに通報することが定められている。

　ちなみに、ペットを勝手に捨てるのは**動物愛護管理法**違反で立派な犯罪。100万円以下の罰金が科せられる。

　問題なのは、**無許可**で危険動物を飼うケースも増加していることだ。

　2005年9月に埼玉県上尾市で捕獲されたニシキヘビの飼い主は、届け出をしていなかったため**書類送検**されている。やはり肝心なのは飼い主のモラルだろう。

all cases the owners are required by law to promptly inform authorities if these animals escape.

Even with dogs and cats, simply abandoning a pet is a serious crime under the **Animal Protection Act**, and subject to a fine of up to ¥1 million.

The real problem, however, is that cases of people keeping "controlled animals" without proper authorization are also on the rise.

In September 2005, the owner of a python was prosecuted for failing to report to authorities when the animal escaped. Toughening enforcement is fine, but the pet owner's own sense of responsibility is what really seems to be at the heart of the matter.

ちぎれた1万円札、銀行で交換してくれるのか？

　半分にちぎれた1万円札。銀行に持っていくと新札に交換してくれるのか。その場合、"半分"だから5000円？　それともまるまる1万円？

　半券でも1万円札に交換してくれるとしたら、1枚の1万円札が2万円に化ける。**そんなうまい話はないだろう**と思いながら、試しにほぼ半分にちぎれた万札の半券を銀行に持っていくと——引き換えられたのはやはり5000円札だった。

　ところで「半分」で5000円なら、「3分の1」ではいくらになるのだろう。3000円か？　窓口の女性に尋ねてみたが、「3分の1という基準はございませんで、3分の2か5分の2になります」と要領を得ないので、日本銀行に問い合わせてみた。

　「破れたり燃えたりした**銀行券**は、表・裏両面があることを条件に、面積基準で新しい銀行券との引き換えを行っています。残存面積が3分の2以上あれば全額、5分の2以上、3分の2未満の場合は半額として引き換えしております」（日本銀行政策広報部）

　面積が5分の2に満たなければ、銀行券としての価値はなく、失効してしまうそうだ。当然ながら、1万

Can you really exchange a torn ¥10,000 bill at the bank?

If you take a torn half of a ¥10,000 bill to the bank, will they exchange it for a new bill? Since it's torn in half, will you only get ¥5,000, or a full ¥10,000?

If you were able to get a bank note of the same value for the torn half of a bill, we'd all have an easy way to double our money, and **that sounds a little too good to be true**. Just to try it out, we took the larger portion of a ¥10,000 bill torn nearly in half to the bank for exchange... And what do you think we got? ¥5,000.

So if we get ¥5,000 for half of the bill, could we get ¥3,000 for a third of the bill? All the **teller** was able to tell us was, "There's no standard for one-third of a bill, only two-thirds and two-fifths." So we went to the Bank of Japan to find out more.

"The rules for exchanging burnt or torn **bank notes** depend on the surface of the bill which is still intact. Both the face and reverse of the notes also have to be identifiable. For a remaining surface area of 2/3 or more, the damaged bill is replaced at face value. If the remaining surface area is between 2/3 and 2/5, half of the original value is given.

If the remaining surface area is less than 2/5, it's considered worthless money and you're out of luck. So naturally,

円札をどのように分割して引き換えても、満額の1万円を超えないように設定されているのだとか。これらの基準は、日本銀行のホームページhttps://www.boj.or.jp/about/services/bn/sonsyo.htmの「損傷銀行券の引換基準」というコーナーでも詳しく図解で説明されている。

　ちなみに、燃えて灰になっていても、その灰が日本銀行券ということが確認できれば、引き換え基準の面積に含めてくれるそうだ。しかし、灰になると面積は目減りするのでは？

「日本銀行券は紙質が良いので、燃えてもほとんど原形をとどめたまま黒く炭化します。**縮み度合いも僅少で、専用の鑑定盤に載せても、通常の紙幣とさほど差がありません**」（日本銀行発券局）

　灰になったり汚損度合いが激しいと、普通の銀行の窓口では受け付けてくれないことが多いが、全国の日本銀行の窓口まで持っていけば、どんな状態でも鑑定してくれるそうだ。

they have the rules set so that you could never exchange the damaged bill for more money than you started out with. The rules are explained in detail (with pictures) on the Bank of Japan's homepage under "Criteria for Exchange of Damaged Banknotes" (https://www.boj.or.jp/about/services/bn/basic/sonsyo.htm).

Even if your money gets completely burnt, as long as they can confirm that the ashes are those of Bank of Japan notes, they'll count the charred surface area toward your exchange. But won't the surface area have shrunk after the bill is burnt?

"The paper we use for bank notes is of extremely high quality; and even when burned, it usually just chars, keeping its original shape. **Shrinkage** is also minimal. Even when placed on the templates used to appraise the surface area, the difference in area for burnt bills isn't very significant at all."

When bills have been burnt or severely damaged, your local bank is less likely to be willing to exchange them, but you can always get them appraised at any of the Bank of Japan branches throughout the country.

なぜペットボトル入りの牛乳はないのか?

　ジュースやお茶など、**ペットボトル入りの清涼飲料**は、いまや**当たり前**。しかし、ペットボトルの牛乳は見かけない。どうしてだろう?

「**乳製品**の衛生基準を定めた乳等省令で、牛乳の容器はガラス瓶か**紙パック**と決められているため、ペットボトルは使用できないのです」

と言うのは、日本乳業協会。大手牛乳メーカーの答えも、判で押したように同じだった。

　乳等省令の制定は昭和27(1952)年のこと。当時、**栄養価が高い乳製品**は主に病院食として使われていた。そのため、清涼飲料と違って厳しい**衛生基準**が必要だったという。

　しかし、ペットボトルが不衛生だというわけではない。省令ができた時代に、ペットボトルが存在しなかっただけのことだ。厚労省としては牛乳メーカーから申請を受ければ省令の改正を検討する余地もあるという。

　現に、フルーツ牛乳やヨーグルトなどは、申請を受けてペットボトルの使用が認められ、すでに商品化されている。軽いうえに、落としても変形しにくいペットボトルはやはり便利だ。

日本の生活のギモン ● **Problems with Daily Life**

Why don't they sell milk in plastic bottles?

For tea and other soft drinks, **plastic bottles** have become the **norm**. But why do we never see milk in plastic bottles?

According to Japan Dairy Industry Association, "The Ministerial Decree on Dairy Products, which dictates health regulations for **milk products**, states that the only containers to be used for milk are glass bottles and **paper cartons**. Plastic bottles aren't allowed." The answer we got from a leading milk producer was exactly the same, as though they were reading it off the same page.

The Decree was established in 1952. In those days, milk products were mainly used in hospitals because of their **high nutrient content**, hence the strict **hygiene regulations**.

But there's nothing unhygienic about plastic bottles. It's just that they didn't exist at the time the law was drafted. The Ministry of Health Labour and Welfare has the authority to investigate changing the law if requested to do so by milk producers.

And that's exactly what has happened with products like fruit-flavored milk and yogurt drinks. The manufacturers requested an investigation, and the use of plastic bottles was approved. This makes production much easier, as plastic

なのに牛乳については、どのメーカーも認可を申請していない。その理由を大手メーカーに尋ねて、ようやく聞けた理由はこんなものだった。

「牛乳は雑菌が繁殖しやすいので、ペットボトル化するには『一度口をつけたら残さないで』『常温で持ち歩かないで』と注意する必要がある。また、新たな設備投資や紙容器より高いペットボトルのコストアップの問題もあるし、認可申請の手続き上、安全性の実証データも提出しなければならないんですよ」

　いろいろ面倒な問題があるようだ。もっと頑張ってもらいたいものだが……。

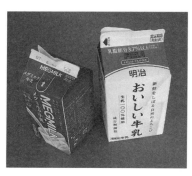

牛乳の容器といえば紙パックかガラス瓶
Milk comes in paper cartons or glass bottles.

bottles are light weight and highly resistant to shock.

But in the case of ordinary milk, no company has requested a change in the law. Another milk producer we asked was finally able to give us the answer why.

"Bacteria can grow very rapidly in milk, so to put it in plastic bottles, we'd have to warn customers not to leave any left over if they drink it directly from the bottle, and not to carry it around with them all day. Higher costs due to investment in new equipment needed to use the more expensive plastic bottles are also a problem. And to get an investigation going, we'd have to submit detailed data establishing the safety of using plastic bottles..."

Excuses, excuses! The biggest problem seems to be that switching to plastic bottles would be a pain in the ass for the dairy industry. We hope they're at least a little more enthusiastic when it comes to making milk!

緊急車両は任意保険に入っているの?

パトカーや救急車でも事故を起こすことがある。はたして緊急車両は任意保険に入っているのだろうか?

「消防・救急合わせて1848台の車両があります。当然、**自賠責保険**は全車加入ですが、任意保険には1台も入っていません」

というのは東京消防庁。数字は2006年2月時点のものだ。自賠責の限度額を超えた損害は消防庁が自己負担で賠償する。

「年間の事故は、**軽い接触**も含めて10件前後です。車両数が多いので、保険なしで賠償したほうが安いんですよ」(同広報)

警視庁(東京都)も全車未加入だが、警察・消防とも全国一律の基準はなく各都道府県ごとに事情が異なる。例えば埼玉県や沖縄県では全車両が任意保険に加入しているという。

加入して保険料を払う場合も、未加入で賠償を自己負担する場合も、財源は税金。国民にとっても安

日本の生活のギモン ● **Problems with Daily Life**

What kind of insurance do emergency vehicles have?

There's no guarantee that police cars and **ambulances** won't cause traffic accidents of their own. So how are **emergency vehicles** insured?

"There are 1,848 cars in our facility. Of course, we have **liability insurance** for all of them, but there's no coverage beyond the minimum requirements for even a single car," an official from the Metropolitan Fire Department said. If the mandatory insurance can't cover the full damages of an accident, the department bears the responsibility.

"In a given year, only around 10 accidents occur, including **light collisions**. It is less expensive for us to pay damages on a case-by-case basis rather than increase insurance coverage because we have too many cars," explains Department public relations.

The Metropolitan Police Department doesn't insure any of its vehicles beyond minimum requirements either, but there is no national standard, so the insurance requirements differ from one prefecture to the next. For instance, in Saitama and Okinawa, all public vehicles must be insured beyond minimum requirements.

Regardless of whether they buy extended insurance coverage or pay compensation without insurance, the money

いほうがありがたいが、実際のところ、どちらが安いのだろう。

　2001年の埼玉県議会資料によると、任意保険加入以前の県警車両の事故による**賠償額**は、年間500万〜1000万円。加入後の年間保険料は1000万円強。必ずしも自己負担のほうが安いとは言いきれない。

　「保険未加入でも役所が賠償してくれるなら安心」とも言えない。被害者は役所相手に、保険会社抜きで自力交渉をしなければならないのだ。多額の賠償は自治体の議会承認が必要なため、支払いが遅れることもある。

　保険未加入のパトカーに関してこんな話も。
　「**公務中**の事故でも、警官個人が**被害者**に賠償金を払って済ませることがある。実はこのカネの出どころは警察がプールしている裏金という説もあるんです」（事情通）。事実なら、"裏の保険"もあるってことか？

is coming out of tax-payer's pockets. From a citizen's point of view, the cheaper, the better; but which method is actually cheaper?

According to documents from the Saitama prefecture assembly in 2001, yearly **compensation** for police cars' accidents ranged from 5 to 10 million yen before they began insuring the cars. After introducing insurance, the premiums cost ¥10 million a year or more. Still, it can't necessarily be said that it is always less expensive to pay compensation without extra insurance.

It's also perhaps naive to assume that without extra insurance, "there is no problem because the government will pay." Victims have to negotiate with the government directly, not via insurance companies. Also, payment may be delayed because approval of compensation has to make its way through local councils and a good deal of red tape.

Another story about police cars and "insurance." "Even if an accident occurs while they are **on duty**, sometimes the officer tries to take care of things by compensating the **victims** privately. It's rumored that the money comes from a secret fund which the police keeps under the table," one insider said. If that's true, it means that the police may be guilty of some crimes of their own when it comes to handling taxpayer's money.

ざるそばはノリをのせただけで なぜあんなに高いのか？

ざるそばといえば、たいていは、もりそばにノリをのせただけなのに50〜100円も高かったりする。たかがノリだけで、なぜこうも値段が違うのか。

「ざるそばは、ほかのそばよりも高級なメニューとして江戸時代に生まれました。値段の差はその**名残**です」と言うのは、全国麵類文化地域間交流推進協議会。当初のそばは現在のもりそばに当たるが、ゆでずに蒸したもので、菓子屋が売る安価な間食メニュー。一方、ざるそばは、麵打ち技術や**高級食材**の発達で江戸中期に生まれた、オシャレなゆでそばだ。「ざるの元祖が、深川洲崎の伊勢屋です。良質のそばを使い、**竹ざるの器**の目新しさで評判になりました。やがて、当時は高級品だったみりんを汁に使う店やノリをのせる店も現れて、ざるそばにさまざまな**付加価値**がついたんです」（そば研究家・笠井俊彌氏）

後に従来のそばが、ざるやかけと区別して「もり」

日本の生活のギモン ● **Problems with Daily Life**

Why is *zaru soba* so expensive when it's only garnished *nori*?

Come to think of it, *zaru soba* is nothing more than mori soba (basic chilled soba noodles served on a flat basket or a plate) with a little bit of *nori* (dried seaweed) sprinkled on it. Yet it costs ¥50 or ¥100 more than a regular bowl of chilled soba. Why does just a little *nori* change the price like this?

"*Zaru soba* was born during the Edo period as a more exclusive alternative to other *soba* dishes, and the difference in price is a **reflection** of this," says the All-Japan Noodle Cultural Exchange Promotion Council. Originally "*soba*" was just *mori soba*, except that the noodles were steamed, not boiled—a cheap snack sold at candy shops. On the other hand, *zaru soba* was born in the middle of the Edo period as a fashionable boiled soba dish, boasting developed kneading techniques and **expensive ingredients**. "The first shop to make *zaru soba* famous was "Iseya" in Fukagawa-suzaki. They developed a good reputation because they used high quality *soba*, and served it in a stylish **bamboo sieve**. Later, some shops started to use *mirin* (sweet sake), a luxury during the Edo period, in the *soba tsuyu* (dipping sauce) or garnishing the dish with *nori*. Thus, *zaru soba* came to have **extra perceived value**," *soba* researcher Toshiya Kasai told us.

Later, regular *soba* started to be called *mori soba* to

と呼ばれるようになり、オプション付きの「ざる」と、オプションなしの「もり」という区別が完成した。

「しかしいまは、両者の違いはノリだけという店が多い。効率化のほか、みりんやワサビが安価で手に入るようになって、もりにもざるにも使われ始めたからです」（そば業界関係者）

こうして、ざるの**特別感**が薄れ価格差だけが残ったというわけだ。しかし、ざるの「付加価値」に**こだわる**店は今もある。日本橋「室町砂場」のざるは、もりと違い、そばの実の芯だけを使う白麺で100円増。「神田まつや」は、天城の本ワサビ付きで150円増。「本物のざる」には、今もノリ以外の高級な付加価値がちゃんと付いているのだ。

純粋に「ノリ代」なのか？
Is *nori* all this comes with?

distinguish it from *zaru soba* and *kake soba* (hot *soba* in broth topped with thinly sliced scallion), and the difference eventually came to be perceived as *zaru soba* having toppings, and *mori soba* not.

"However, nowadays, many diners consider the *nori* garnish to be the only difference between the two dishes. Also, as *mirin* and *wasabi* are much cheaper these days, the *nori* is one of the few things left to justify the higher price," one *soba* manufacturer told us.

Thus, the **exclusiveness** of *zaru soba* faded away but the price difference remained. However, some diners **are** still **particular about** the "added value" of *zaru soba*. Muromachi Sunaba in Nihonbashi serves *zaru soba* made from only hearts of *soba* grain and it's ¥100 yen more expensive than their *mori soba*. Kanda Matsuya uses *Amagi Wasabi* and charges ¥150 more. So maybe "real *zaru soba*" has not only *nori* but also a little extra perceived value as well.

日英対訳
日本のギモン
Street Smart Trivia

2015年12月7日　第1刷発行

編　者　　日刊ゲンダイ
訳　者　　ジョンソン スティーヴンリン

発行者　　浦　　晋亮

発行所　　IBCパブリッシング株式会社
　　　　　〒107-0051 東京都新宿区中里町29番3号
　　　　　菱秀神楽坂ビル9F
　　　　　Tel. 03-3513-4511　　Fax. 03-3513-4512
　　　　　www.ibcpub.co.jp

印刷所　　株式会社シナノパブリッシングプレス

© 2015 Nikkan Gendai
© 2015 IBC Publishing
Printed in Japan

落丁本・乱丁本は、小社宛にお送りください。送料小社負担にてお取り替えいたします。
本書の無断複写（コピー）は著作権法上での例外を除き禁じられています。

ISBN978-4-7946-0389-0